❧ CONTENTS ❧

INTRODUCTION

You can always tell the time of year just by walking through a fabric shop. Holiday prints and seasonal fabrics are everywhere. Our senses are infused with valentine hearts, Easter bunnies, Mother's Day bouquets, Fourth of July prints, Halloween pumpkins, Thanksgiving turkeys, and festive Christmas and Hanukkah designs. These special fabrics are vibrant, colorful, richly patterned, and widely available. Fabric shops stock these wonderful holiday prints months before the actual holiday to give you plenty of time to design festive quilts. But how can you use all of these marvelous fabrics in your quilts? Let them inspire you, spark your imagination, and set your creativity in motion! In short, you can create holiday collage quilts.

Holiday Collage Quilts is a follow-up to my first book, *Fabric Collage Quilts* (That Patchwork Place, 1999), which is about using fabric motifs to create easy and dramatic quilts. *Fabric Collage Quilts* also explores uses for the many wonderful and interesting fabrics that are readily available to today's quilter.

The first part of *Holiday Collage Quilts* is an overview of the basic techniques used to create a collage quilt. If you are familiar with *Fabric Collage Quilts,* you'll find that there are several new techniques in *Holiday Collage Quilts,* including dimensional appliqué, padded appliqué, layering, and using computer-generated clip-art images to print your own holiday fabrics. In addition, I share new ideas for embellishing your projects with polymer clay, beaded lettering, beaded fringe, and holiday trims.

In the second part of this book, you will find complete directions for eight holiday quilts. These festive projects are fun, easy-to-complete quilts that will dress up your holiday celebrations and make wonderful and memorable gifts. The directions will guide you through the process of collage quilting. Suggestions are included with each quilt for fabric and embellishing choices. However, these are just suggestions. Look for fabrics that inspire and delight you. Use the patterns as a guide and let your own theme fabrics guide the design for your quilt. Your holiday collage will be original and unique based on your own fabric and embellishing selections.

I know that you will have fun making these lively, colorful, and easy quilted collages. Using fabric motifs makes it easy to create dynamic quilts. So check out your local fabric shops for wonderful holiday designs. Experiment with new fabrics and learn to take design risks. That's what creating art is all about!

Any of the quilts in this book can be embroidered and embellished using your sewing machine. Many newer models have excellent, built-in blanket stitches and machine embroidery options, as well as endless decorative stitch choices. Any or all of these options will add wonderful details to your work.

Personally, I prefer to work by hand. All of the backgrounds for the quilts in this book were pieced by machine. However, all of the appliqué, blanket-stitching, embroidery, embellishing details, and quilting were done by hand. The reason is simple: I enjoy handwork and do not get the same satisfaction from my quilting when I work by machine. I love the feel of my quilt when I am working on it. This is a personal choice. Making quilts should be a comfortable and enjoyable process, so if machine work is your thing, go for it. You can be successful at collage quilting whether you like to do handwork, stitch by machine, or use a combination of techniques.

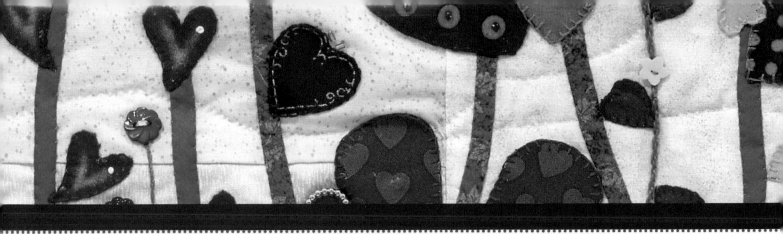

HOLIDAY COLLAGE QUILTS

JOANNE GOLDSTEIN

Martingale™
& COMPANY

ACKNOWLEDGMENTS

Once again I would like to extend my deepest thanks and appreciation to everyone at Martingale & Company for their continued support. Special thanks to Mary Green, Terry Martin, and Karen Soltys for their advice, expertise, and shared excitement about the never-ending possibilities of collage quilting.

A loving and heartfelt thank you goes to my family for knowing when to step back and give me the time, space, and solitude to quilt, write, and create.

Finally, thank you to all of the wonderful quilters that I have met who eagerly share my enthusiasm for this technique. You inspire me!

CREDITS

President . . . . Nancy J. Martin
CEO . . . . Daniel J. Martin
Publisher . . . . Jane Hamada
Editorial Director . . . . Mary V. Green
Editorial Project Manager . . . . Tina Cook
Technical Editor . . . . Karen Soltys
Copy Editor . . . . Ellen Balstad
Design and Production Manager . . . . Stan Green
Illustrator . . . . Laurel Strand
Cover and Text Designer . . . . . Jennifer LaRock Shontz
Photographer . . . . Brent Kane

That Patchwork Place® is an imprint of Martingale & Company™.

Martingale & Company
20205 144th Avenue NE
Woodinville, WA 98072-8478 USA
www.martingale-pub.com

Printed in China
06 05 04 03 02 01   8 7 6 5 4 3 2 1

MISSION STATEMENT
We are dedicated to providing quality products and service by working together to inspire creativity and to enrich the lives we touch.

Library of Congress Cataloging-in-Publication Data

Goldstein, Joanne.
    Holiday collage quilts / Joanne Goldstein.
        p.   cm.
    ISBN 1-56477-359-0
    1. Patchwork—Patterns. 2. Quilting—Patterns.
    3. Appliqué—Patterns. 4. Holiday decorations. I. Title.

TT835 .G656 2001
746.46'041—dc21
                                                    2001030968

....

Making collage quilts is one of the easiest ways to create dynamic quilts quickly with colorful and impressive designs. The following list of supplies will help you get started with your own collage quilts. This is a basic list of the supplies that you should have on hand before you begin your quilt. All of the quilts in this book are accompanied by a detailed list of the supplies that you will need for each quilt.

Basic quilting supplies: You'll need the following items for all of the projects in this book.
- Sewing machine for piecing. Make sure your machine is clean, in good working order, and has a new needle.
- Rotary cutter, mat, and ruler
- Sewing shears
- Pins
- Small appliqué scissors

Threads: Use cotton or cotton-covered polyester sewing thread in your machine for piecing. Try using a medium gray thread in both the top needle and bobbin for all your machine piecing. Neutral gray blends beautifully with most fabric, so it eliminates the need to change thread colors frequently.

Embroidery floss: For regular hand appliqué of images such as vases, stems, and trees, one strand of embroidery floss in a quilting needle makes a neat and invisible appliqué stitch. The floss is soft, easy to sew with, and sinks into the background fabric with a slight tug. It is available in such a wide variety of colors that it is easy to match any fabric closely. Be sure to match your floss to the piece being appliquéd rather than to the background fabric.

Thread for blanket stitch embroidery: Embroidery floss is also perfect for blanket stitch embroidery. However, there are many other options. Experiment with variegated floss, metallic floss, rayon and silk threads, perle cotton, narrow silk ribbon, and machine embroidery threads. Try to purchase floss and threads at the same time as your fabric so that you can easily match, coordinate, and contrast colors. Combine different threads in the same quilt for variety, texture, and interest.

Thread Heaven or beeswax: Using metallic threads for hand embroidery can be a challenge, since they tangle, fray, and break easily. Thread Heaven is a silicone thread conditioner that you can use to coat metallic threads to make them stronger and less likely to tangle and fray while embroidering. It comes in a little box and you simply run a length of thread over the substance before stitching. Beeswax can also be used to condition metallic threads.

Sequin pins: For all appliqués use tiny, ½" sequin pins. Although it can take time to get used to these tiny pins, I think you'll find that they work great for appliqué. They remain securely pinned into the fabric and do not get in the way during the appliqué process. Try them! Of course, for piecing your quilt background, you'll still want to use regular straight pins.

Fusible web: There are several different, easy-to-use brands of paper-backed fusible web on the market. Choose a lightweight fusible web that will be easy to embroider through. It is very important to follow the manufacturer's instructions for fusing the fabric to ensure a secure bond. If in the handling of the quilt top some of the fused pieces become loose, simply readhere them with a hot iron.

Embroidery hoop: I find an 8" size works best since it is large enough to encompass most motifs and small enough to manipulate comfortably in your hands. You can use either a wood or plastic hoop with a tightening screw. Some embroidery hoops have spring tension instead of a tightening screw. Generally, hoops with a tightening screw hold fabric more securely and your work is less likely to slip during embroidery, but either type will work.

Silk ribbon: Use silk ribbon to add details such as leaves, small flowers, grass, stems, and foliage. Try 4mm, 7mm, and 13mm widths for a variety of different accent sizes on your quilt.

Beads: Use seed beads to add finishing touches to flower stamens and buds, to highlight specific areas, and to add sparkle to your quilts. In addition to seed beads, experiment with bugle beads and other flat and faceted beads. Almost any kind of bead will work on a collage quilt. If you haven't used beads on your quilts before, try it. I'm sure you'll be delighted at the surface texture and tiny details they can add.

Beading thread: Use Nymo or Silamide thread to secure all beadwork. This strong thread will keep small seed beads securely in place. Look for this thread in the beading section of most craft stores.

Needles: You'll need a variety of hand-sewing needles if you plan to embellish your quilt by hand, as I do.
- Embroidery needles in size 7 or 8
- Chenille needles in various sizes to fit your threads
- Quilting needles in a size that is comfortable for you to use (for hand appliqué and hand quilting). It is helpful to use a size 8 needle for hand quilting through the motif portions of the quilt. Smaller needles can break easily when quilting through multiple layers.
- Size 10 quilting needles. Long, slender beading needles are sometimes difficult to use when attaching beads to a quilt. They bend and break easily, and it is not necessary to use such long needles. Instead, you can use a size 10 quilting needle to attach beads to a quilt. Most beads easily fit through this needle, which is less likely to bend or break than a beading needle.

Fabric stiffener and small paintbrush: You will need to stiffen some of the fabric motifs for dimensional appliqué. Several fabric stiffening products are available, and they can usually be found with the glue products in most fabric and craft shops. Look for a water-based formula for easy clean up. Purchase a small, inexpensive paintbrush to apply the stiffener to the fabric motifs.

Bleached muslin: Keep white muslin or other solid white cotton fabric on hand for printing graphics and clip art from your computer to the fabric.

Bubble Jet Set or artist's permanent spray fixative: If you want to print clip-art images onto fabric to use in your quilt, you can use Bubble Jet Set or spray fixative to help set the ink into the fabrics. Bubble Jet Set can usually be found at quilt shops, and your local shop may order it for you if they do not carry it. Artist's spray fixative is available at arts and craft stores.

Freezer paper: For tracing patterns and stabilizing fabric for computer printing, nothing beats freezer paper.

Iron and Teflon press sheet (optional): Fusible web can be rough on your iron. Even careful pressing can result in small pieces of fusible web sticking to the bottom of your iron. Using a Teflon press sheet can help keep your iron and ironing board free from the sticky residue.

Paper scissors: You'll need paper scissors for cutting out freezer-paper shapes and fusible-web pieces. Save your good scissors for cutting fabric.

Bias bars: Using bias bars to make long bias strips is a fast, easy, and precise method.

Water-soluble pen: I like to use this type of marking pen to draw embroidery designs on a quilt top. The marks are easy to see and will remain on the quilt until washed out. Be careful not to press any marks with an iron before washing them or they may not wash away.

Chalk pencil: Use a white chalk pencil to mark designs onto dark fabrics. Be sure to use a chalk pencil instead of one that contains wax so that you can easily brush away marks.

Batting: Choose a thin, flat batting with a very low loft, or try lightweight fleece.

Embellishments: Collect buttons, charms, sequins, lace, and ribbons. It is easy to find embellishments with holiday themes. Almost any item that can be sewn down can be used in collage quilting. Using these embellishments in your quilts will add texture and interest to your work.

FABRICS

As with any quilt you make, your fabric choices are the key to a beautiful collage quilt. You'll need to choose three basic types of fabrics: your background fabrics, the all-important holiday theme fabrics, and the fabrics for the additional appliqué pieces that tie a design together. Start with the holiday theme fabrics, because you'll want to make your background and appliqué fabric choices based on what you plan to include as the main focus of your quilt.

HOLIDAY THEME FABRICS

The most important fabrics you will need for holiday collage quilting are the theme fabrics. The theme fabrics that you choose will make your quilt a unique and personal design. Theme fabrics are prints with large (at least 2" to 3"), well-defined motifs that can be easily cut out from the fabric. In collage quilting, these motifs are used as the major design element in the quilt. Finding holiday theme fabric is so easy. Almost all fabric shops stock a large selection of holiday fabrics that generally have large, colorful, and eye-catching images that are fun and easy to work with. Many stores feature these fabrics well in advance of the actual holiday. It is not unusual to see poinsettias and Christmas holly fabric in July, and Easter bunny fabric popping up while the snow is still on the ground. It is never too soon to start to think about your next holiday quilt!

Holiday theme fabric is colorful, vibrant, and very easy to find.

The amount of theme fabric to purchase depends on the size of the motifs and how often they repeat. As a general guide, if a motif is 1" to 2" in size and repeats closely, half a yard will be enough. You'll need to cut out the design motifs with a ¼" seam allowance. If the design motifs are so close together that they touch each other, some motifs will be unusable so you will need to purchase additional yardage. If the motifs are large—3" or more—and spaced 3" or more apart, you will need to purchase approximately one yard of fabric. As you purchase your theme fabrics, keep in mind how many of the specific motifs you plan to use in your quilt and purchase accordingly.

Searching for and collecting theme fabrics is fun. It is even more fun to use these wonderful fabrics in your quilting. Check your own fabric stash. You may already have several holiday fabrics that you have purchased in the past but didn't quite know how to use in your quilting. Now is the time to dig these fabrics out of the closet. You will be amazed at how quickly and easily wonderful quilt designs will come together using holiday theme fabrics.

In addition to theme fabrics with holiday motifs, look for other types of theme fabrics that you can incorporate into your quilts. Look for floral patterns, butterfly motifs, birds, leaves, sun and moon motifs, clouds, small insects, and animals. Consider anything that will enhance your designs and add interest to your projects. The most successful collage quilts are designed with a variety of motifs pulled from many different fabrics, so you'll want to have several theme fabrics on hand to help you design your quilt. Try to purchase fabrics with different size motifs for variety and eye appeal. It will be easier to add perspective, depth, and diversity to your design if you have different image sizes to work with.

Motifs on a light background stand out easily.

SECRETS FOR SUCCESS

Most of the theme fabrics you find will be 100 percent cotton. However, if you find other types of fabrics such as decorator prints, silk, rayon, and blends that just happen to have the perfect pictures, buy them! Since you will be cutting out the motifs and fusing them to the background, you can successfully use many types of theme fabric in your quilts; the fusible web gives even loosely woven or stretchy fabrics the stability needed for appliqué.

Motifs on a dark background can be bold and dramatic.

BACKGROUND FABRICS

In addition to theme fabrics, you'll also need fabrics for the background of your quilt. Many of the holiday quilts in this book have pieced backgrounds. Look for subtle prints for the background. Keep in mind that small-scale prints in the background complement large-scale motifs in the foreground. By varying the print scale between the background and the printed motifs, you are ensuring a successful quilt that is not too busy yet has great visual interest. You do not want the two sections of the quilt to compete with each other visually.

Use 100 percent–cotton fabric for all background piecing. Try to purchase your theme fabric first so you can choose background colors and prints to complement the motifs. Aim for contrast between the two parts of your quilt. Dark backgrounds highlight the fabric picture and create excellent impact. Light backgrounds are calm and subtle, allowing the picture to be the main focus of the work. Either approach can produce dramatic effects.

APPLIQUÉ FABRICS

While the holiday motifs will become the main focus of your quilts, you will need other 100 percent–cotton fabrics for appliqué. Notice that the quilts include appliqué shapes, such as a basket or a birdhouse, that are larger than the holiday motifs and form the basis of the design. In the project directions, you'll find yardage requirements for these appliqué fabric pieces, but you may want to vary your color choices based on the holiday theme fabrics you choose. Most of these appliqué pieces are small and don't require a lot of fabric, so you may already have what you need on your fabric shelves or even in your scrap basket. When you choose these "supporting player" fabrics, you may want to look for prints or patterns that mimic real-life designs, such as a small-scale plaid to emulate a basket-weave design. Try to keep the patterns subtle and smaller in scale than your holiday motifs so these appliqué shapes don't overwhelm the real "stars" of the show.

·: BASIC COLLAGE TECHNIQUES ·~

The following are the basic technique instructions for all of the quilts in this book, from fusing shapes and appliquéing them, to simple embroidery techniques. If collage quilts are new for you, I suggest you read through the techniques before starting a project. If you're already familiar with this style of quilting, you may want to refer to this section merely as a refresher.

HAND APPLIQUÉ

Most of the quilts in this book have several hand-appliquéd pieces that form the basis of the overall design. These pieces are generally appliquéd first, before adding all the theme fabric motifs, but refer to the individual project directions for specific instructions.

Using the patterns that accompany each quilt project, trace the appliqué shapes onto the dull side of freezer paper to make appliqué templates. (Note: Some pattern pieces are too large to fit on one page. You'll need to join the individual pieces, such as A-1 and A-2, to make your templates.) Cut out the templates on the drawn lines. With your iron, press the freezer-paper template to the *right side* of the appliqué fabrics you've selected. Cut out the appliqués, leaving a ¼" seam allowance beyond the edge of the freezer paper. Pin the appliqués to the background, following the placement diagrams. Then, using the freezer paper as a guide, turn the seam allowance under along the edge of the paper with your needle, and appliqué the piece in place with a blindstitch.

If you prefer to use freezer paper on the *wrong* side of the fabric, reverse the printed pattern before tracing it onto your freezer paper. Press the freezer paper to the wrong side of the fabric. Using your needle to turn the seam allowance over the edge of the paper, begin to appliqué the piece. When you have about 1" of the appliqué edge left to stitch down, carefully remove the freezer paper from behind the appliqué, fold under the seam allowance, and complete the stitching. To make hand quilting easier, cut away the background fabric from behind large appliquéd shapes.

BIAS STRIPS FOR STEMS AND MORE

Several of the quilts require the use of bias strips for stems, branches, basket handles, and other design elements. I find using bias bars is the quickest and easiest method for making perfect bias strips.

1. Start with ½ yard of fabric and fold a corner diagonally as shown.

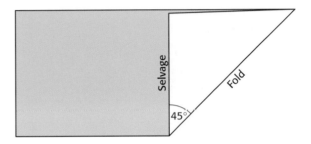

2. Lightly press the crease. Open the folded fabric and use a ruler and rotary cutter to cut 1"-wide bias strips parallel to the crease.

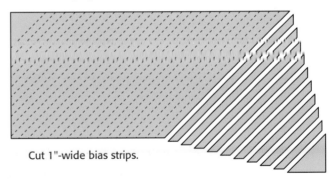

Cut 1"-wide bias strips.

3. Fold each bias strip in half lengthwise, with *wrong* sides together. Determine the desired bias-strip width and stitch that far from the folded edge of the strip. For example, if the finished bias strip needs to be ¼" wide, stitch ¼" from the folded edge. Trim the seam allowance close to the stitching. Insert a bias bar into the resulting tube and turn the tube until the seam allowance falls along the center back of the bias bar. Press the tube flat; then remove the bias bar and press again.

FUSING

Fusible web makes it easy to secure many different fabric motifs to your quilt. There are several brands of fusible web on the market. Just be sure that the one you purchase is lightweight and has a removable paper backing. If the product says "heavy-duty" or "no-sew" on the package or bolt, you won't be able to embroider through it. Save the plastic information sheet with the manufacturer's instructions that accompanies your fusible web, and refer to it when necessary.

From the theme fabric, cut out motifs approximately ¼" beyond their edges. Then cut out the motif shapes from the fusible web, following the general outline of the motifs that includes the extra fabric ¼" around the edges. Press and adhere the fusible web to the wrong side of the motifs, following the manufacturer's directions. Here's where a Teflon pressing sheet comes in handy! Use the pressing sheet underneath the fusible web to protect the iron and ironing board. Then cut away the excess ¼" of fabric from the motif edges, following the exact outline of the motifs. Carefully remove the paper backing by scoring the paper with a pin. The paper can then be peeled away easily. Continue this procedure until all the motifs have been fused to the fusible web.

Choose a fabric motif, fuse the fusible web to back, cut along the edge of motif, and remove the paper backing.

Pin the prepared motifs in place on the quilt top. When all of the motifs are pinned in place and you are happy with the design, fuse them to the quilt top.

EMBROIDERING MOTIFS

When you are ready to embroider around the edges of the motifs, begin in the center of the quilt top. Place the quilt top in an 8" embroidery hoop. Thread an embroidery needle with two strands of embroidery floss, metallic floss, rayon floss, or one strand of perle cotton or other decorative thread. Using a blanket stitch, embroider around each motif. Be sure to keep your stitches evenly spaced as you embroider.

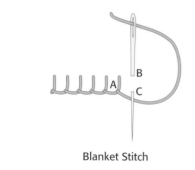

Blanket Stitch

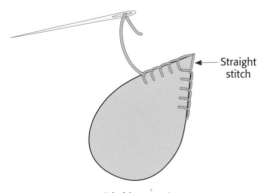

Straight stitch

Stitching a Point

EMBELLISHING WITH EMBROIDERY

You can easily add details to your work by learning a few simple embroidery stitches. Using two strands of embroidery floss and the stem stitch, embroider long, fluid stems to anchor leaves and buds. Use perle cotton and the feather stitch to embroider ferns between some of the flowers. Try French knots as flower stamens, and the backstitch to embroider delicate tendrils and vines.

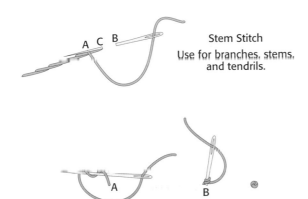

Stem Stitch
Use for branches, stems, and tendrils.

French Knot
Use for flower centers, water bubbles, and highlights.

Backstitch
Use for small twigs, trailing lines, and outlines.

Feather Stitch
Use for sprays of foliage, small branches, and as a filler in floral designs.

SILK RIBBON EMBROIDERY

Using silk ribbon for embroidery stitches, you can add wonderful, dimensional enhancements to your quilts. Use narrow silk ribbon (4mm) to add embroidered French knots, leaves, and tiny buds to stems and vines. Wider sizes (7mm and 13mm) are perfect for adding accents like embroidered flowers and leaves.

Silk ribbon is delicate and frays easily, so use short lengths (10"–12") at a time to avoid fraying. Use a chenille needle for ribbon work. Follow the diagram below to thread and knot the ribbon.

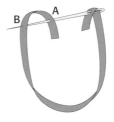

Making a Knot

Following the stitch diagrams below, practice silk ribbon embroidery. Keep your stitches loose and even. The ribbon may tend to twist during embroidery. Untwist the ribbon and try to keep it as flat as possible to produce even, beautiful stitches.

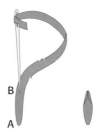

Japanese Ribbon Stitch
Insert needle at point B; then pull gently until ribbon curls at edges.

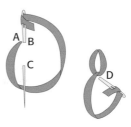

Lazy Daisy Stitch

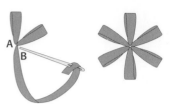

Loop Flower

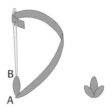

Rose Bud
Make a small straight stitch;
then make a second stitch over
the first to create a padded bud.
Make 2 straight stitches at the bottom
of the padded bud for leaves.

Spider Web Rose
Use 1 strand of floss to form spokes,
then weave ribbon over and under
until the spokes are covered.

ADDITIONAL EMBELLISHMENTS

While embroidering your holiday motifs to the quilt top gives it added dimension and texture, there's no need to stop there! You can further enhance the look of your special holiday collage quilts by adding beads, buttons, charms, or other treasures. Take a look in your sewing box or at your local craft or fabric shop for the perfect accents for your quilt.

Beads

Beads are excellent embellishing accents that add highlights, dimension, sparkle, and impact to quilts. Beads can be used as flowers or flower centers. They can add starlike accents to evening skies and can be used to indicate twigs, leaves, and buds. Beads can be grouped in clusters, sewn on individually, or strung on thread and couched onto your quilt for different effects. Beads are versatile because they come in a wide selection of colors, sizes, and shapes. To attach beads to your quilt, use a size 10 quilting needle with beading thread such as Nymo or Silamide. These special beading threads are quite strong, so you can securely attach beads to your project without fear of them breaking and sending your beads scattering.

To sew your beads to the quilt top, thread your quilting needle with a length of beading thread that has a knot at one end. Bring the needle up through the back of the fabric, load on as many beads as you wish, and then return the needle into the fabric close to the first stitch. Continue sewing on beads in this manner, taking the time to make a knot at the back of the fabric after every fourth or fifth stitch. This will secure the beads and prevent an entire line of beads from falling off if the thread should break. For ideas on using beads for fringe and lettering, see page 17.

Use colorful beads to add highlights and sparkle to your quilt.

Buttons

Buttons are another excellent embellishing accent. They are available in a wide selection of sizes, colors, and shapes in just about every craft and fabric store. Visit the button department of your favorite shop and you will see buttons made from plastic, leather, wood, metal, stone, and fabric. Some craft stores sell bags of interesting, assorted buttons at very reasonable prices. Some buttons are flat with holes that make attaching them to your quilt simple. Others have shank backs. If you prefer the button to lie flat on the quilt, simply snip off the shank with a wire clipper. You can then glue the button on with a drop of white tacky glue.

Buttons are a great source of creative embellishing. Begin to collect interesting buttons as well as those with holiday themes so you will have a varied selection to choose from when embellishing your work.

Interesting buttons can add texture and pizzazz to your quilt.

Charms

Charms can add a delightful touch to your quilt. Like buttons, charms are available in many different sizes and designs. Commonly available in gold- and silver-toned metal, you'll also find these whimsies made of plastic, porcelain, and wood. Use them to highlight and add theme definition to your quilt. Charms with holiday themes are readily available in most fabric and craft shops. Search out charms such as hearts, bunnies, flags, pumpkins, and Christmas flowers to add to your holiday quilts.

Inexpensive charms are another way to add dimensional details to your collage.

NEW TECHNIQUES FOR
~ HOLIDAY COLLAGE QUILTS ~

You will find many new and exciting techniques used in *Holiday Collage Quilts* to add even more texture, dimension, and interest to your work. After all, making a collage means using a wide variety of techniques, embellishing goodies, and additional surface details. It is a combination of numerous techniques that will make your holiday collages interesting and unique. Read through the directions for each of these techniques to determine which ones you'd most like to include on your projects. The specific project directions will refer you to the techniques I used to make each quilt pictured in the book.

DIMENSIONAL MOTIFS

Using dimensional motifs in your collage will give your quilt wonderful surface texture and visual impact. Adding dimensional motifs invites closer scrutiny and makes your work interesting and unique. Choose several large motifs from your theme fabrics for dimensional work. Flowers, butterflies, birds, and leaves all look wonderful using dimensional techniques. Try using some of your holiday motifs such as hearts, flags, and pumpkins as your dimensional motifs. Attach fusible web to the back of each motif as described in "Fusing" on page 10. Then fuse each motif to a piece of coordinating fabric, either a solid or print. Trim the motifs along the exact edge of the design. Use a small blanket stitch to cover the raw edges of the fused motifs. Stitch all the way around each motif, covering the edges and hiding the beginning and ending knot in the center of each motif. (Take a tiny stitch through the back layer only, which will keep the knot hidden in the center so it won't be visible when the motif is attached to the quilt.)

Embroider a small blanket stitch around the outside of the motif.

Hide the beginning and ending knots in the center back of the motif.

After you've embroidered all of the dimensional motifs, you'll need to coat them with a liquid fabric stiffener, which gives the motifs extra body and stiffness and helps raise them from the surface of the quilt, thereby adding a dimensional element to your work. The following steps describe how to apply the fabric stiffener.

1. Pour a small amount of fabric stiffener into a shallow dish.
2. Using a small, inexpensive paintbrush, paint the prepared motif with the fabric stiffener. Use long, even strokes to cover the entire surface of the motif. The stiffener will coat the motif with a cloudy liquid. This liquid will dry clear and the motif will become stiff. Usually one coat of stiffener is enough to add just the right amount of body to the motif.
3. You can easily shape the motifs while they are still wet. Bend butterfly and bird wings forward, shape curved petals, and so on.
4. Allow the stiffened motifs to dry completely (about one hour) before attaching them to your quilt top.

Fabric stiffener will help the motifs hold their dimensional shapes.

To attach dimensional motifs to the quilt, simply take a few stitches in the center of the motif to secure it to the quilt. You may also use beads or a small button in the center to attach the motifs. The edges of the motifs aren't sewn to the quilt, so they can stand up and away from the surface of the quilt to add an extra, interesting and textural design element.

LAYERING

You can also use embroidered and stiffened dimensional motifs to add layering effects to your quilt. Layer the stiffened motifs directly over identical motifs that have been blanket stitched to your quilt top to add perspective and movement to your quilt. For example, butterflies seem to be flying when the motifs are layered, flower petals appear to be blowing in the wind, and birds are about to take flight. Layering is an easy and wonderfully creative way to make your quilts dynamic.

Dimensional motifs add texture to the quilt top, "popping" right off the surface.

Layering a dimensional motif over an identical flat motif helps add movement to the design.

PADDED MOTIFS

Padding motifs is another way to add a bit of dimension subtly to your quilt.

1. Cut a piece of lightweight fleece or low-loft batting about ¼" smaller than the motif you want to pad. Place the fleece under the prepared motif and fuse the motif to the quilt top.
2. Embroider the edges of the padded motif to the quilt top with a blanket stitch.

The subtle padded effect will add a soft dimensional quality to the motif. When you combine dimensional motifs, layering, and padded motifs, your holiday collage quilts will become more interesting and visually exciting.

Pad some motifs with low-loft batting for subtle dimension.

COMPUTER CLIP ART

Computers give us a whole new way to add interesting motifs and details to our quilts. You may be able to find free clip art on the Internet, or you can purchase clip art computer programs that offer thousands of images from which you can choose. If you cannot find just the right motifs from your theme fabrics, search for an appropriate clip art image on your computer. Using your computer lets you change the size and color of an image. You can rotate and flip images, and you can combine several images to create unique fabric—just one more creative way to enhance your collage quilts.

Printing a clip art graphic on fabric is easy. However, the ink from your printer probably isn't permanent and is likely to run if the fabric gets wet. There are several ways you can treat the fabric to lessen the chance of this from happening. The first method is to pretreat the fabric with a product called Bubble Jet Set (available in quilt shops and through mail-order catalogs). By soaking solid white fabric or muslin in this liquid before printing, the ink from your printer will set permanently into the fabric. The fabric remains soft and easy to work with. Soak about one yard of white, tightly woven, 100 percent–cotton fabric (200 thread count is ideal) or bleached muslin fabric in the Bubble Jet Set liquid. Completely saturate the fabric and let it sit in the liquid for about five minutes. Remove the fabric from the liquid and hang it up to air dry completely.

Once you have chosen a graphic or clip art, print out a sample on paper. Make sure that the size, color, and orientation of the graphic are right. Cut a piece of freezer paper to the exact size of your printer paper, which is generally 8½" x 11". Trim your pretreated fabric approximately ¼" smaller than the freezer paper. Iron the fabric to the shiny side of the freezer paper. Make sure the fabric is tightly and evenly attached to the freezer paper, with no loose areas, wrinkles, or frayed threads along the sides. Now simply place into the printer tray the prepared fabric that is adhered to the freezer paper, and print. Allow the ink on the printed fabric to dry completely. Then peel off the freezer paper, rinse the fabric in warm water with mild soap, and allow it to dry. Once the fabric is printed with your computer-generated motif, use it the same way you would any theme fabric that you have chosen for your quilt.

Another less-permanent way to help set the ink from your printer into the fabric is to spray the fabric with artist fixative (available in any art supply store) after the image is printed onto the fabric. Spraying the fabric with fixative will help preserve the color and help control bleeding of the ink if the fabric becomes wet. However, fixative may not make the ink completely permanent. If you plan to wash your quilt, make a sample print on the fabric to test the ink's reaction to water.

Look for clip-art graphics that you can print on cotton to add to your theme fabrics.

COUCHED THREADS, RIBBONS, AND TRIMS

Heavier decorative threads, ribbons that are narrow and flat, and a variety of interesting trims can be used in collage quilts to add another element of surface texture. Use a tiny straight stitch, a whipstitch, French knots, beads, or small buttons to attach these threads and trims in place on the quilt. This process is called couching. Wind them through floral and landscape designs to suggest foliage, grass, and ferns. If you prefer to do your work by machine, you can use invisible thread in the needle and a long zigzag stitch to sew over ribbons and trims and attach them to your quilt top.

Couch interesting threads and ribbons with beads, tiny buttons, a whipstitch, or a straight stitch.

Try couching different kinds of trims, including a string of beads.

BEADED FRINGE AND BEADED LETTERING

An easy way to add sparkle and texture to quilts is to use beaded fringe and lettering. While the results can be dazzling, beads are simple to use, readily obtainable, and available in a variety of colors, shapes, and sizes.

When adding beaded fringe to a quilt, begin the work after the entire quilt is finished, including all quilting and even the binding. Thread a size 10 quilting needle with beading thread and make a small knot at one end. Bring the needle through the back of the quilt, close to one corner, and exit the quilt at the exact corner of the binding. Pull firmly so that the small knot pops through the fabric and is buried in the batting. Pick up as many beads on your needle as necessary to create approximately 1½" of fringe. Pull the needle through all the beads. Then, skipping the last bead that you put on the needle, put the needle back up through the row of beads and pull firmly on the thread (but not so tightly that the row of beads buckles). Bring the needle through the binding, close to the first row of beaded fringe. Slide the needle through the inside of the binding, parallel to the bottom edge of the quilt. Bring the needle out through the bottom of the binding, about 1" away from the first row of fringe. Pick up beads and repeat for each row of fringe across the bottom of the quilt. When you reach the other end of the quilt, secure the thread with a small knot, and end the stitching by popping the knot through the back of the fabric.

Stitching words, sayings, and names to your collage quilt is a way to add meaning to your project, and you can add these sentiments with pizzazz when you spell them out with beads. This type of beading is done before you layer and baste your quilt. Using a water-soluble pen, carefully trace or write the words onto your quilt. You can use a light box or window to transfer the lettering to your quilt, or just write it freehand. Place the quilt top into an embroidery hoop to stabilize the fabric. Thread a size 10 quilting needle with beading thread and knot the end. Come up through the back of the fabric and pick up 3 seed beads. Go down through the fabric, pulling firmly so that the beads lie flat against the fabric. Come up between the first and second bead as shown. Insert needle through the second and third beads. Pick up three more beads and repeat this process, following your marked line. End the thread by stitching into the fabric and securing the thread with a small knot close to the fabric.

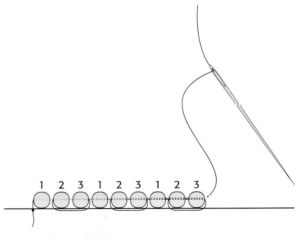

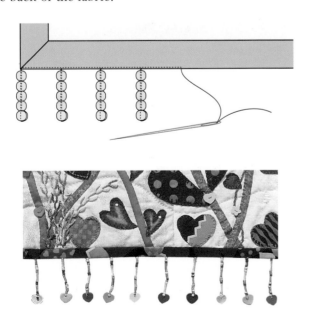

Beaded fringe is easy to do and adds a touch of whimsy to your quilt collages.

Lettering is another way to add beads to your quilt.

POLYMER CLAY ACCENTS

Finding just the right embellishing accent for your quilts can sometimes be a challenge. But with polymer clay, you can easily create your own tiny flowers, leaves, hearts, stars, and other three-dimensional details. Polymer clay is available in a wide range of colors at most craft and hobby stores. Once you've conditioned (or softened) the clay, it can be baked in a home oven, making it an easy and fun product to use. Polymer clay is non-toxic and safe to use. However, once an item such as a cookie sheet or rolling pin comes into contact with the clay, do not use it for food preparation.

Polymer clay is fun and easy to work with to create interesting items for embellishing.

To use polymer clay successfully, you first need to spend a few minutes conditioning or softening it. The easiest way to condition polymer clay is to roll it in your hands for several minutes. Friction, as well as body heat from your hands, will soften the clay and make it pliable. Once the clay is conditioned, break off a small piece and practice molding it into different shapes.

The simplest way to make embellishing accents for your quilts is to look for shape cutters and molds made especially for polymer clay. You can also use small canapé cutters (found in stores that carry cooking supplies). Roll out a thin, flat sheet of clay using a rolling pin, brayer, or pasta machine. Remember, though, that once you use any of this equipment, you must dedicate it solely for use with clay; no more homemade pasta!

Press the cutters into the clay to make all kinds of shapes. Ovals and teardrops make perfect leaves. Just lightly score vein lines with a straight pin. Stars and flowers make wonderful sky embellishments. Several tiny hearts combined together make great flowers; hearts cut from green clay can also be used as leaves.

In addition to using cutters, it is very easy to mold the clay into simple shapes. Roll a small piece of clay in your hands and shape it into an oval. Flatten the oval between two fingers, taper one end to a point, and score with a straight pin. You have perfect leaves! Tiny, round polymer clay beads make wonderful flower centers and buds. Use a straight pin or toothpick to pierce a hole into the clay shape before you bake it so you can easily stitch the clay to your quilt top.

Practice making clay beads and buttons for your collage quilt.

To cure or harden the clay shape, place it on a baking tray and bake according to the package directions. Be careful not to overbake the clay. It can burn easily. Once the clay items have cooled, you can sew them to your quilt.

It is easy to mold or cut interesting leaves, flowers, and other shapes from polymer clay to add to your quilt.

Musical notes made with polymer clay add the perfect songbird accent.

"WHERE'S THE WORM?"

One day while I was working on a quilt for my first book, my 14-year-old son David walked into the room. He noticed a small green worm that I was using to embellish a tropical landscape design. "Mom," he said, "I love the worm! It's the best part of your quilt!" A few weeks later, I was working on another quilt, when David once again appeared. "Mom, where's the worm? You should put a worm on every quilt that you make."

I thought about David's comment and realized that it was not too often that my teenage son paid any attention to anything that I was doing. I decided to hide a worm somewhere on every quilt that I do. It has become a fun tradition between us. My quilts are never complete until David asks, "Mom, where's the worm?"

"Where's the worm?"

HELPFUL HINTS

Here are my top-ten tips for fabric collage quilts. Follow these hints, and you're sure to be successful with all of your projects!

1. To separate strands of embroidery floss, cut a piece about 12" long. Grasp it in the middle and gently pull the strands from the skein.

2. Use ½" sequin pins when pinning motifs to the quilt. These tiny pins hold securely and can be ironed over without damaging your iron or your fabric.

3. Always allow the fused motifs to cool before removing the paper backing. To remove the paper backing, gently score through it with a pin and remove.

4. If the fused motifs become loose while embroidering, simple re-adhere them with a hot iron. It is helpful to leave the pins in place after fusing to secure the motifs until they are embroidered.

5. Always cut away the background fabric from behind the appliquéd pieces such as vases and trees. This step will eliminate the bulk of an extra layer and make hand quilting much easier. These instructions refer only to appliquéd pieces that are not fused; they do not refer to fusible theme-fabric motifs. Never try to cut away the background fabric from behind fused motifs.

6. Unless the motif is black, do not embroider around it with black thread. Your stitching will look like a coloring book outline.

7. Change colors as you blanket stitch around the motifs. Follow the colors as they change on the fabric to give depth and dimension to your work.

8. When cutting out a small group of flowers, leaves, or petals, you don't have to cut out each motif individually. You may cut a small group of images as one piece. But remember to embroider around each flower and leaf separately.

9. If your needle bends or breaks while you are embroidering, it is probably too small for the job. Switch to a slightly larger needle to accommodate the threads you are using. (The lower the number, the larger the needle.)

10. Always use an embroidery hoop to do all embroidery and embellishing work on your quilt.

·:· FINISHING THE QUILT ·~·

Your appliquéd, embroidered, and embellished quilt top is beautiful. But let's face it; it's not a quilt until it's quilted and bound. Perhaps you want to add borders, or you may want to move right to quilting, binding, and attaching a hanging sleeve. Whatever your fancy, this section will help you turn your project into a completed work of art.

PRESSING

Carefully press the quilt top with a dry, warm (not hot) iron. Cover your ironing surface with a thickly folded towel so you won't flatten your quilt. Be especially careful when pressing near silk-ribbon embroidery—you don't want to squash the stitches as you press. Similarly, be careful around beadwork and other embellishments. You don't want to crush any three-dimensional features or snag the iron on beads, buttons, or other attachments.

After pressing, make sure all four sides of the quilt are straight and even, since they may have distorted slightly due to the embroidery. Before adding borders or layering and basting, square up the corners and straighten the sides, if necessary, with your rotary cutter and ruler.

BORDERS

Borders frame the quilt and give it a finished look. However, many quilts can stand on their own without borders. This is especially true of contemporary designs. The border colors should complement the quilt top, and the size should be in proportion to the rest of the quilt. On quilts that measure between 50" and 60", a 4" border gives a neat, framed finish. Attaching a narrow inner border (1" to 1½" wide) is like adding a mat to a painting before it's framed.

On heavily appliquéd, embroidered, and embellished quilts, a simple border is usually the most effective. An elaborately pieced border would compete with the rest of the quilt top. If the border seems overly plain, let some small appliquéd and embroidered motifs spill over from the quilt onto the border for a more unified look.

You can opt for either mitered or straight-cut corners. Miters make the border look more like a picture frame, but both styles have their places.

Measuring for Borders

To keep your quilt square, it's critical that you measure the quilt top before you add the borders. Measure the quilt top through the center in each direction—width and length; don't measure along the edges. If you're adding multiple borders, measure after each addition.

For straight-cut borders, measure the quilt top and cut borders to fit two opposite sides of the quilt. After attaching these borders, measure the quilt top again, including the borders you just added; then cut the next two borders to that measurement. Don't stitch longer border sections to the quilt top and trim later. Stitching before trimming makes it easier for your quilt to stretch out of shape.

For mitered borders, you need to cut strips longer than the quilt sides. Measure the quilt top through the center to determine the quilt-top dimensions; then add 10" to that measurement. Cut your border strip to that length. If you're adding multiple borders, you can stitch all the borders for one side of the quilt together before adding them to the quilt top. Fold the borders in half to find the center and mark with a pin. Match the border's center to the center edge of the quilt top. Pin the border to the quilt top and stitch, starting and stopping ¼" from each end of the quilt. Repeat for all four sides of the quilt.

At the ironing board, fold back one end of a border at a 45° angle and press. Pin in place. At the sewing machine, open the fold and sew the borders together, stitching on the crease.

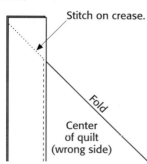

Stitch on crease.

Fold

Center of quilt (wrong side)

Stitch all four corners in the same manner. Trim the excess fabric, leaving a ¼" seam allowance. Press the seam allowances open.

BATTING

Choose a thin, flat batting for your quilt. Wall quilts should lie flat, and puffiness will detract from the dimensional effects you stitched into the surface. In addition, if you plan to hand quilt, remember that some portions of the quilt (the fused motifs) consist of multiple layers. The thinner the batting, the easier it will be to quilt through. Consider separating a low-loft batting into two layers for a very soft, thin, and easy-to-quilt "sandwich." Lightweight fleece, which is sold by the yard, is also an excellent choice.

LAYERING AND BASTING

If your quilt is larger than 40" in both directions, you'll need to piece the backing fabric. Purchase enough fabric for two lengths of the quilt. Cut the fabric in half, trim the selvages, and then sew the two pieces together side by side. Press the seams open for easier quilting. Trim the pieced backing so it's approximately 3" larger than your quilt top. Save the excess fabric to make a hanging sleeve.

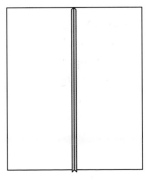

For large quilt backings,
sew fabric lengths together.

Lay the backing fabric on the floor or table, right side down. Place the batting over the backing, then add the quilt top, right side up. Baste the three layers together securely with white thread or with safety pins.

QUILTING

Begin quilting in the center of the quilt top on one of the printed motifs. Quilt on and around the motif, following the design on the fabric. For example, if the motif is a flower with leaves, quilt on the lines that indicate the petals and leaf veins. Add quilting accents to all the motifs. As you quilt, you will notice that the design becomes much more three-dimensional.

You can finish your quilt with either machine or hand quilting—or try a combination of both. If you choose to machine quilt, consider hand quilting the motif sections and machine quilting the background. If you decide to machine quilt the entire quilt, use free-motion quilting so that you can move easily around the design. Be careful to avoid quilting over any embellishments you may have added.

Once all the motifs are quilted, move on to the pieced background. Simple quilting, such as grids, diagonal lines, and in-the-ditch stitching are usually most effective. Simple, traditional quilting in the background enhances the more complex quilting and embellishing in the appliqué design.

When all the quilting is completed, trim the batting and backing fabric even with the quilt top. Once again, check that the quilt is square and hasn't distorted during quilting. Square up the quilt if necessary by trimming it with your rotary cutter and ruler.

Quilting adds the final embellishment to
your motifs—and the whole project.

ADDING A HANGING SLEEVE

Using leftovers from the quilt backing, cut a piece of fabric 8½" wide by the width of your quilt. Turn the short edges under ¼", then turn them under again. Stitch the fold in place to hem the edges.

Fold the fabric in half so that the long, raw edges meet. Press. Pin or machine baste the hanging sleeve to the back of the quilt, aligning the raw edges of the sleeve with the raw edges of the top of the quilt. The raw edges will be enclosed in the binding.

Hand sew the folded edge of the hanging sleeve to the quilt back with a blindstitch. Stitch through the batting and backing for extra security.

Baste sleeve to top edge of quilt.

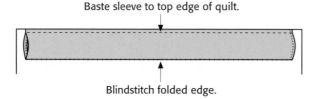

Blindstitch folded edge.

BINDING THE EDGES

Cut enough binding strips to go around the perimeter of your quilt, adding about 5" extra for mitering the corners. You can cut strips anywhere from 2" to 2¼" wide, depending on how wide you prefer your finished binding. Since your quilt has thin batting, narrow binding may be appropriate.

Stitch the binding strips together end to end with diagonal seams to make one continuous strip.

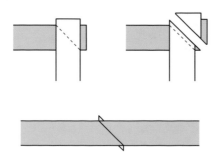

Fold the strip in half lengthwise and press. Using a ¼" seam allowance, stitch the folded strip to the right side of the quilt top using a walking foot.

To miter the corners, stop stitching ¼" from the corner. Clip the threads and fold the binding at a 45° angle.

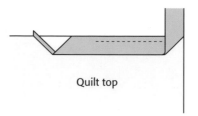

Quilt top

Fold the binding back down, flush with the edge of the quilt as shown. Begin stitching the binding to the next side of the quilt. Repeat for each corner.

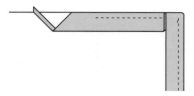

When you reach the starting point, overlap the ends of the binding and stitch in place.

Fold the binding to the back of the quilt and hand stitch in place.

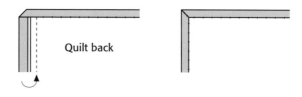

Quilt back

THE QUILTS

On the following pages you will find complete directions for eight holiday collage quilts. Remember that these directions are only suggestions. Your quilts will be a unique and individual expression based on your own specific theme-fabric choices. You can easily adapt any of the designs for whatever theme fabrics you choose. Several of these quilts can also be altered to reflect other holidays. For example, you can transform the quilt "For Mother" into a Thanksgiving quilt by filling your basket with fall flowers, leaves, and harvest fruits and vegetables. Similarly, the couple sitting on the front porch in "Let Freedom Ring" could just as easily be looking out over a pumpkin patch, springtime garden, or snow-covered Christmas trees. By using lovely tulips, daffodils, lilies, and bunnies in place of cats, "Garden of Hearts" could become a charming Easter garden. Just remember that by using theme fabrics, you can easily create a unique, personal, and creative holiday collage quilt.

Detail from "Garden of Hearts"

GARDEN OF HEARTS

GARDEN OF HEARTS BY JOANNE GOLDSTEIN, 2000, CORAL SPRINGS, FLORIDA, 41" X 29".

As February approaches, our thoughts turn to hearts, valentines, and love. Collect as many heart fabrics as you can find and plant your own romantic garden. This nontraditional Valentine's Day wall hanging will cheer the winter blues and brighten any wall with year-round color, whimsy, and fun. When your own garden of hearts is in full bloom, embellish it to your heart's content!

MATERIALS

Note: All fabrics are 100 percent–cotton quilting fabrics unless otherwise specified. All measurements are based on 42"-wide fabrics.

¼ yd. (or fat quarters) *each* of 9 assorted light neutral fabrics such as tone-on-tones and pale subtle prints for background

8" x 8" square of black-and-white check for sleeve

8" x 10" scrap of yellow fabric for glove

⅜ yd. blue fabric for watering can

¼ yd. dark blue fabric for watering can handle, spout, top, and trim

½ yd. dark green fabric for stems

1½ yds. fabric for backing and binding

1½ yds. low-loft batting for padded motifs and quilting

Water-soluble marker

Freezer paper

8" embroidery hoop

1 yd. fusible web

THEME FABRICS

Note: Measurements are approximate; be sure to purchase enough fabric for several repeats of each motif.

You'll need approximately ½ yard each of assorted valentine hearts and other heart fabrics. Choose several different heart motif sizes for variety and dimension. Look for colorful, patterned heart motifs. Also look for prints of small birds, butterflies, ladybugs, and other insects. I added two small, whimsical cat motifs to my garden, too.

Fabric suggestions

EMBELLISHING SUPPLIES

Embroidery floss, perle cotton, rayon floss, metallic floss, variegated embroidery thread, or decorative threads of your choice in assorted colors

Decorative heart, flower, and butterfly buttons

Seed beads in assorted colors, Nymo beading thread, and size 10 quilting needle for attaching beads

Heart, musical note, and other charms

Polymer clay beads

Package of red seed beads for lettering

Optional: If you wish to add beaded fringe, you will need about 40 tiny heart charms (or make your own from polymer clay) and additional seed and bugle beads.

Embellishing suggestions

CUTTING FOR BACKGROUND

Cut rectangles as indicated in the following list from the 9 light neutral fabrics for a scrappy, pieced background.

From *each* of fabrics 1 and 2, cut:
   1 rectangle, 8½" x 21½"

From *each* of fabrics 3 and 4, cut:
   2 rectangles, 8½" x 10"

From *each* of fabrics 5 and 6, cut:
   2 rectangles, 8½" x 7"

From *each* of fabrics 7 and 8, cut:
   1 rectangle, 7" x 19½"

From fabric 9, cut:
   1 rectangle, 5½" x 13½"

PIECING THE BACKGROUND

Lay out all the light neutral rectangles as shown in the diagram below. Then join the rectangles together as shown, starting with the *a* seam, followed by the *b* seam, and so on.

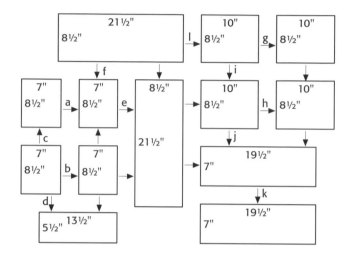

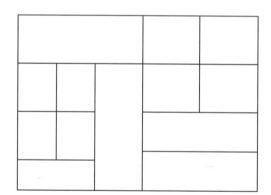

APPLIQUÉ

1. Before appliquéing any pieces, use a water-soluble marker and the pattern on page 73 to trace the words "love grows here" onto the quilt top. Use the color photograph on page 24 and illustration below as placement guides.

2. Following the directions in "Hand Appliqué" on page 9, trace each "Garden of Hearts" pattern piece on pages 70–72 onto freezer paper. Using these freezer-paper templates, cut out each piece from your selected fabric.

3. Following the photograph on page 24 and the illustration below, appliqué each piece in place in the following order:
   - Sleeve (A) from black-and-white check fabric
   - Glove (B) from yellow fabric
   - Watering can (C) from blue fabric
   - Handle (D and E) from dark blue fabric
   - Spout (G) from dark blue fabric
   - Watering can top (F) from dark blue fabric

4. Cut a 1½" x 9½" strip from the dark blue fabric and appliqué it in place across the watering can for trim.

5. Use 2 strands of black embroidery floss and the stem stitch to outline the entire glove. Use a running stitch (indicated by ----- on the pattern) to add stitching details to the glove.

6. Referring to the directions for "Bias Strips for Stems and More" on page 9, make ¼" bias strips as follows from the dark green fabric: six 20"-long strips, three 15"-long strips, eight 10"-long strips.

7. Appliqué the bias strips in place for stems, using the photograph and illustration as placement guides.

FUSING THE GARDEN MOTIFS

1. Referring to "Fusing" on page 10, cut out motifs from your theme fabric and apply fusible web.

2. Referring to the quilt photograph, begin to place the motifs on the quilt top. Place hearts along the stems made with bias strips. To add depth and perspective to the design, allow some of the hearts to overlap and move off the edges of the quilt. Place small birds on several of the stems. Cut several of the larger hearts in half to work as colorful leaves and place them along the stems. Add small butterflies and insects to the garden. Continue to add motifs from your fabrics to fill the design. Use clusters of smaller hearts to create blossoms at the top of some of the stems. Place a large heart motif in the center of the watering can lid as a knob. Pin all of the motifs in place.

3. Following the directions in "Padded Motifs" on page 15, choose several of the large hearts and pad them with batting for dimension.

4. When you are pleased with the arrangement of the motifs and the design of your quilt, fuse all the motifs in place with a hot iron.

EMBROIDERING THE MOTIFS

Refer to the directions in "Embroidering Motifs" on page 10, and use the color photograph as a placement guide for all embroidery accents. Blanket stitch around all of the fused motifs. Remember to change colors and use different types of thread as you embroider the various hearts.

EMBELLISHING YOUR DESIGN

1. Referring to "Embellishing with Embroidery" on page 11 and "Additional Embellishments" on page 12, have fun adding details to your quilt. To begin, use the outline stitch to suggest small branches along the stems.

2. Use the featherstitch to indicate bushes growing at the bottom of the quilt.

3. Choose several small heart buttons to add to the trim of the watering can. Use buttons to indicate tiny flowers and buds along the stems. Add seed beads to highlight some of the hearts.

4. Add seed beads to the padded appliqué hearts. By sewing the seed beads through the padded motif, the heart will become more dimensional.

5. Attach musical note charms or buttons near the birds, and tiny heart or flower buttons to the ends of some of the featherstitches. Or, you can make your own accents using polymer clay (see page 18).

6. Referring to the directions in "Beaded Fringe and Beaded Lettering" on page 17, use a beading thread such as Nymo to attach red seed beads along the marked lines for lettering.

7. After quilting your project and attaching the binding, add beaded fringe to the bottom edge. Refer to the directions on page 17.

8. Remember to sign and date your work of art!

SUNRISE IN THE CARROT PATCH

SUNRISE IN THE CARROT PATCH BY JOANNE GOLDSTEIN, 2000, CORAL SPRINGS, FLORIDA, 34" X 33".

Finally the ice begins to melt, the sun begins to warm the earth, and our thoughts turn to spring. Easter is in the air, and you are ready to make a quilt to celebrate the joyous rebirth of the season. Here in the carrot patch, the sun is rising, the crops are sweet and tender, and the bunnies are everywhere! Celebrate the season with this small wall hanging that will delight and charm your holiday guests.

MATERIALS

Note: All fabrics are 100 percent–cotton quilting fabrics unless otherwise specified. All measurements are based on 42"-wide fabrics.

¼ yd. *each of 2 light blue fabrics for sky*

⅜ yd. landscape fabric (look for trees, small buildings, or farmland)

¼ yd. light green fabric for farmland and vines

¼ yd. bright yellow fabric for sun

½ yd. white fabric for fence

½ yd. white print for border

⅜ yd. brown fabric for tree branches

1½ yds. fabric for backing and binding

1 yd. low-loft batting

Freezer paper

1 yd. fusible web

8" embroidery hoop

THEME FABRICS

Note: Be sure to purchase enough fabric for several repeats of each motif.

Look for holiday and spring motifs such as bunnies, carrots, baskets, butterflies, vegetables, flowers, small birdhouses, birds, and watering cans. Choose several different motif sizes to add perspective to your work. Remember, you can add to your fabric motifs with computer clip art (see page 15).

Fabric suggestions

EMBELLISHING SUPPLIES

Embroidery floss, perle cotton, rayon floss, metallic
floss, variegated embroidery thread, or decorative
threads of your choice in assorted colors

Seed beads in assorted colors, Nymo beading thread,
and size 10 quilting needle for attaching beads

Decorative buttons and charms such as carrots,
butterflies, and flowers

Polymer clay for making accents such as flowers,
leaves, or carrots

Optional: I attached a carrot garland (found in the
holiday trims section of a fabric or craft store) to
the bottom of my quilt as a fringe. You could also
use a floral or bunny trim.

Embellishing suggestions

CUTTING FOR BACKGROUND

From the first light blue fabric, cut:
    5 strips, 1¾" x 42"
From the second light blue fabric, cut:
    4 strips, 1¾" x 42"
From the landscape fabric, cut:
    1 rectangle, 9½" x 26½"
From the light green fabric, cut:
    1 strip, 4½" x 26½"

PIECING THE SKY BACKGROUND

1. Sew 6 of the 1¾" x 42" light blue strips together
   into 2 different strip sets as shown below: 1 strip
   set with one fabric on the outside (A), and 1 strip
   set with the other fabric on the outside (B).

2. Cut the strip sets into 1¾" segments. Cut 14
   segments from Strip Set A and 7 segments from
   Strip Set B.

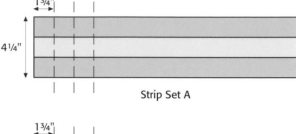

Strip Set A

Strip Set B

3. Join the segments to make 7 Nine Patch blocks
   as shown.

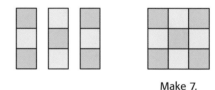

Make 7.

4. Sew the remaining light blue strips together as
   shown below to make another Strip Set B. Cut the
   following segment widths from this strip set and
   the remainder of Strip Set B from step 2.
   • One 4¼"-wide segment
   • Four 8"-wide segments
   • One 15"-wide segment

5. Join the Nine Patch blocks and longer segments from step 4 together as shown to complete the sky background.

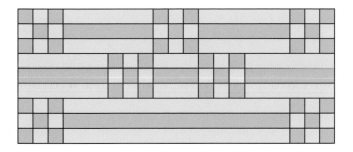

Appliqué detail from "Sunrise in the Carrot Patch"

APPLIQUÉ

1. Following the directions in "Hand Appliqué" on page 9, trace each "Sunrise in the Carrot Patch" pattern piece on pages 74–76 onto freezer paper. Using these freezer-paper templates, cut out each piece from your selected fabric.

2. Following the color photograph and the illustration below, appliqué the A–D sun pieces on top of the blue pieced sky background.

3. Before you appliqué the rest of the pieces, join the sky background to the 9½" x 26½" landscape piece, as shown in the illustration below.

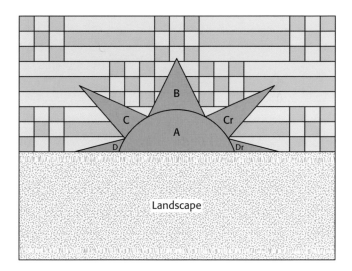

4. Referring to the directions for "Bias Strips for Stems and More" on page 9 and using the white fence fabric, make ½" bias strips in the following lengths: two 26½"-long strips, three 11½"-long strips, two 10½"-long strips, and six 7½"-long strips. Refer to the photograph on page 28 for placement and appliqué the bias-strip fence pieces in place.

5. Join the 4½" x 26½" light green strip to the bottom of the pieced sky and appliquéd landscape unit to complete the background.

6. Before you can appliqué the tree-branch pieces (E and F), you'll need to attach the border to the quilt. Refer to "Finishing the Quilt" on page 20. Measure the length of your quilt. From the white-print border fabric, cut 2 strips, 4½" wide by the quilt length measurement. Sew the 2 border strips to the sides of the quilt and press the seams toward the border strips. Then measure the width of your quilt, including the side border strips. Cut 2 more strips from the white-print border fabric, 4½" wide by the quilt width measurement. Sew the border strips to the top and bottom of your quilt; press.

7. Appliqué the tree-branch pieces to the top left and right sections of the quilt, using the photograph and the illustration below for placement.

8. Make 2 bias strips, each ¼" x 25", from the light green fabric for vines. Arrange the bias-strip vines on the bottom corners of the border as shown, and appliqué them in place.

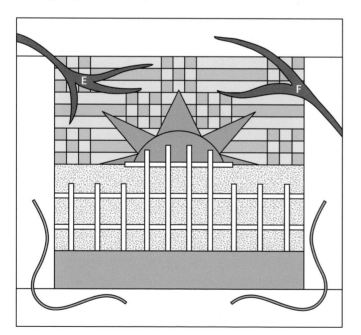

FUSING THE GARDEN MOTIFS

1. Referring to "Fusing" on page 10, cut out motifs from your theme fabric and apply fusible web.

2. Referring to the quilt photograph, begin to place the motifs on the quilt top. Place garden motifs such as carrots, baskets, and a vegetable cart on the landscape background. Let your theme fabrics inspire and guide you as you design your quilt. Add bunnies, birds, a birdhouse, and butterflies to fill your scene. You may wish to place a birdhouse on top of the fence, chicks in the garden, or a basket of Easter eggs on the ground. Choose some small leaves and flowers to climb up the fence. Use lots of larger leaf motifs to fill the branches of the trees. You can even place a small bird's nest and some birds in one of the trees.

3. Add flowers, leaves, carrots, and/or bunny motifs from your theme fabrics along the vines made with bias strips in the lower corners.

4. Continue to add motifs from your fabrics to fill the design. Pin all of the motifs in place. When you are pleased with the arrangement of all the motifs and the design of your quilt, fuse all the motifs in place.

5. Choose some of the motifs for dimensional appliqué and layering. In the sample, the bird at the top and the butterfly at the middle left were layered. The watering can hanging from the fence is padded dimensional appliqué.

EMBROIDERING THE MOTIFS

Refer to the directions in "Embroidering Motifs" on page 10 and use the color photograph as a placement guide for all embroidery accents. Blanket stitch around all of the fused motifs. Blanket stitch around the dimensional appliqué and layered motifs, too. (Layered motifs should not be fused to the quilt top.)

EMBELLISHING YOUR DESIGN

1. Referring to "Embellishing with Embroidery" on page 11 and "Additional Embellishments" on page 12, have fun adding details to your quilt. To begin, use the outline stitch to embroider stems climbing up the fence.

2. With silk ribbon, embroider leaves to the stems.

3. Use the featherstitch to embroider the carrot tops.

4. Add seed beads and French knots to the center of some of the flowers for highlights.

5. Attach dimensional and layered motifs, referring to the directions on page 15. For instance, you can attach with a small running stitch the wing of the bird or butterfly. Remember that the edges of your motifs will remain free of the quilt to add dimension to your collage.

6. Use small buttons such as flowers, carrots, and insects to add texture to the collage.

7. Quilt and bind your project.

8. Optional: I added a row of decorative carrots hanging from the bottom of the quilt. If you want to do a similar treatment, quilt and bind your project first before attaching trim to the bottom.

9. Remember to sign and date your work of art!

Dangling carrots provide a decorative edge.

⸙ FOR MOTHER ⸙

FOR MOTHER BY JOANNE GOLDSTEIN, 2000, CORAL SPRINGS, FLORIDA, 28" X 31".

It's May, and Mom is in our thoughts. She has been your #1 fan, constant supporter, cookie baker, tear wiper, chauffeur, problem solver, listener, and advice giver for all of your life. Now it's your turn to give something to Mom. Make her a quilt! Fill a basket with your mom's favorite flowers for a colorful and lasting reminder of your love and your appreciation for all that your mother means to you.

MATERIALS

Note: All fabrics are 100 percent—cotton quilting fabrics unless otherwise specified. All measurements are based on 42"-wide fabrics.

¾ yd. off-white fabric for background
½ yd. second off-white fabric for background
⅛ yd. beige fabric for background
¾ yd. brown fabric for border and binding
½ yd. brown plaid for basket
⅜ yd. light brown fabric for basket trim
⅛ yd. green fabric for flower stems
10" square of white fabric for note card
1 yd. backing fabric
1 yd. low-loft batting
Freezer paper
1 yd. fusible web
8" embroidery hoop
Water-soluble pen

THEME FABRICS

Note: Measurements are approximate; be sure to purchase enough fabric for several repeats of each motif.

You'll need approximately ½ to ¾ yard of floral fabric such as roses, daffodils, or pansies. Choose your mother's favorite flowers to make a unique, personal quilt. Look for several different motif sizes for interest and dimension. You'll also want fabrics that give you an assortment of leaf and bud motifs.

Fabric suggestions

EMBELLISHING SUPPLIES

Embroidery floss, perle cotton, rayon floss, metallic floss, variegated embroidery thread, or decorative threads of your choice in assorted colors

7 yds. of ⅜"-wide decorative ribbon

1 yd. strand of craft pearls

Seed beads in assorted colors, Nymo beading thread, and size 10 quilting needle for attaching beads

Decorative buttons and charms such as small flowers, leaves, and butterflies

12" of ½"-wide white flat lace

Polymer clay for making accents such as flowers, buds, and leaves

Embellishing suggestions

CUTTING FOR BACKGROUND

From *both* of the off-white fabrics, cut:

  2 strips, 4½" x 42". Cut each strip into 4½" squares. You'll need 16 squares of one fabric and 9 squares of the other.

From the larger piece of off-white fabric, cut:

  2 squares, 7" x 7". Cut each square once diagonally to make 4 corner triangles.

  3 squares, 9" x 9". Cut each square twice diagonally to make 12 side-setting triangles.

From the beige fabric, cut:

  1 rectangle, 4" x 25"

PIECING THE BACKGROUND

1. Set the squares and side-setting triangles together in diagonal rows, as shown in the illustration. Be sure to alternate your 2 off-white fabrics to create a subtle checkerboard pattern. Add the corner triangles last.

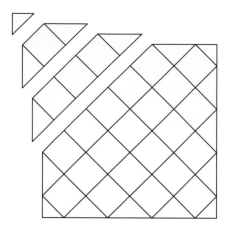

2. Stitch the beige rectangle to the bottom of the pieced background, as shown.

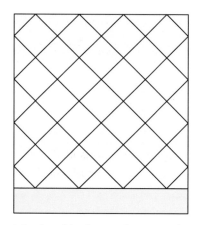

Join pieced background to rectangle.

3. Add a decorative ribbon trim by hand or machine appliqué a ⅜"-wide decorative ribbon over each seam. Weave the ribbon under or over at each intersection. Refer to the color photograph on page 34.

Appliqué detail from "For Mother"

BORDER

Referring to "Finishing the Quilt" on page 20, add a 4½"-wide mitered border. Measure the length and width of the quilt at the centers, and add 10" to each measurement. Trim the border strips to these measurements so you'll have enough length to miter the corners. Sew the border strips to the quilt.

APPLIQUÉ

1. Following the directions in "Hand Appliqué" on page 9, trace each "For Mother" pattern piece on pages 77–78 onto freezer paper. Using these freezer-paper templates, cut out each piece from your selected fabric.

2. Following the photograph on page 34, appliqué the basket (A) cut from the brown plaid.

3. Referring to the directions for "Bias Strips for Stems and More" on page 9, make 2 bias strips from the brown plaid, each ¼" x 35", for basket handles. (Piece strips as necessary.) Pin the bias strips to the quilt, twisting them together as shown in the photograph. Wind the strand of craft pearls through the bias strips, allowing the strand to twist

and turn. Appliqué the bias strips in place for the basket handle. The basket handle will overlap some of the pearls. Use a tiny whipstitch to tack the strand of pearls in place.

4. Make 5 bias strips from the light brown fabric, each ¼" x 7". Appliqué the strips in place on the basket as indicated on the pattern.

5. From the light brown fabric, cut two 1" x 13" strips. Appliqué the strips in place across the bottom of the basket as indicated on the pattern, turning under ¼" along each long edge of the strips. The top strip should cover the raw edges of the vertical light brown bias strips.

6. For flower stems, first make one ¼" x 7" bias strip from the green fabric. Appliqué the bias-strip stem in front of the basket at lower left. Then make several bias-strip stems, ¼" wide and approximately 4" to 6" long, from the same green fabric. Use these stems to anchor some of the flowers in the bouquet. Finally, make 4 more bias-strip stems from the green fabric, each ¼" x 15". Referring to the photograph for placement, appliqué these bias-strip stems in place in the center of each border strip.

FUSING THE FLOWER MOTIFS

1. Referring to "Fusing" on page 10, cut out motifs from your theme fabric.

2. Referring to the photograph of the quilt on page 34, begin to place the motifs on the quilt top. Place flowers, leaves, and buds in the basket. Make your basket lush and full of flowers. Position some of the smaller flowers and leaves so that they spill out over the front and sides of the basket.

3. Place flowers and leaves along the stems made with bias strips.

4. Place tiny flowers, leaves, and buds along the basket handle. Appliqué a single flower to the stem at the bottom of the basket. Add smaller buds and leaves to the stem.

Basket handle detail from "For Mother"

5. Place small motifs along the border stems.

6. Pin all of the motifs in place. When you are pleased with the arrangement of all the motifs and the design of your quilt, fuse the motifs in place.

Border detail from "For Mother"

EMBROIDERING THE MOTIFS

Refer to the directions in "Embroidering Motifs" on page 10, and use the color photograph as a placement guide for all embroidery accents. Blanket stitch around all of the fused motifs. Remember to change colors and use different types of thread as you embroider the various flowers and leaves.

EMBELLISHING YOUR DESIGN

1. Referring to "Embellishing with Embroidery" on page 11 and "Additional Embellishments" on page 12, have fun adding details to your quilt. To begin, use the outline stitch to embroider delicate stems and vines. Refer to the photograph for placement.

2. With silk ribbon, embroider leaves to some of the stems.

3. Use the featherstitch and 2 strands of metallic thread to indicate sprays of foliage.

4. Add seed beads and French knots to the center of some of the flowers for highlights.

5. Use small buttons such as flowers, leaves, buds, and butterflies to add texture to the collage.

6. To make the note card, place the 10" square of white fabric over pattern B. Trace the outside edge of the pattern as well as the words "For Mother," and cut out the rectangle. Referring to the directions on page 17, place the fabric in an embroidery hoop and do beaded lettering.

7. For pattern C, again trace the outside edge of the pattern and the lettering onto the white fabric, and cut out. Use 2 strands of embroidery floss and a backstitch to embroider "Love," and your name.

8. Pin the white flat lace to the front of pattern piece B, keeping the raw edge of the lace and the raw edge of the fabric even. Baste in place. Sew together pieces B and C, right sides together, along the outside edge. Make sure the lettering will face the right direction after the pieces are sewn together.

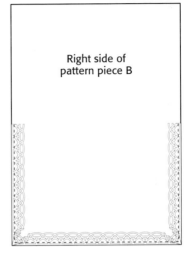

Right side of
pattern piece B

Leave one edge of the note card open for turning, as indicated on the pattern. Turn the note card right sides out and press. Whipstitch the opening closed. Press. Fold in half and press again.

9. Appliqué fabric note card to quilt, referring to the photograph for placement.

10. After quilting and binding, remember to sign and date your work of art!

LET FREEDOM RING BY JOANNE GOLDSTEIN, 2000, CORAL SPRINGS, FLORIDA, 42" X 37".

Capture the spirit of independence with this delightful quilt. You can almost hear the crickets chirping and the fireworks popping as you eavesdrop on this slice of Americana. All across our great country the front porch becomes a front row seat to the dazzling display of lights, noise, and celebration. Let your theme fabric choices help you plan your own version of "Let Freedom Ring."

MATERIALS

Note: All fabrics are 100 percent–cotton quilting fabrics unless otherwise specified. All measurements are based on 42"-wide fabrics.

½ yd. dark blue fabric for evening sky

¼ yd. landscape fabric (look for trees, small buildings, or farmland)

⅛ yd. green print for grass

½ yd. beige print for porch

¼ yd. off-white print for porch posts

Scrap of light floral print for woman's dress

Scrap of plaid for man's shirt

Scrap of skin-tone fabric for hands

Scrap of light print for woman's hat

Scrap of dark brown fabric for man's head

5" square scrap of rust or dark red fabric for flower pots

Scrap of light brown fabric for rug

¾ yd. navy blue fabric for border and binding

½ yd. flag print or red, white, and blue banner fabric for top border

1⅓ yds. backing fabric

1½ yds. low-loft batting

4" x 6" American flag

Freezer paper

1 yd. fusible web

8" embroidery hoop

THEME FABRICS

Note: Be sure to purchase enough fabric for several repeats of each motif.

Look for Fourth of July motifs such as flags, Uncle Sam, stars, eagles, patriotic symbols, and anything that's red, white, and blue. You'll also need other motifs such as flowers, leaves, small strawberries, a cat or dog, and whatever strikes your fancy.

Fabric suggestions

EMBELLISHING SUPPLIES

Embroidery floss, perle cotton, rayon floss, metallic
floss, variegated embroidery thread, or decorative
threads of your choice in assorted colors

Red and white seed beads, Nymo beading thread, and a
size 10 quilting needle for attaching beads

Gold and silver seed and bugle beads

Buttons with a patriotic theme such as flags and stars

Embellishing suggestions

CUTTING FOR BACKGROUND

From the dark blue fabric, cut:
 1 rectangle, 12" x 34½"
From the landscape fabric, cut:
 1 rectangle, 5½" x 34½"
From the green print, cut:
 1 rectangle, 3½" x 34½"
From the beige print, cut:
 1 rectangle, 8½" x 34½"

PIECING THE BACKGROUND

As shown in the diagram, join the rectangles to make the
appliqué background.

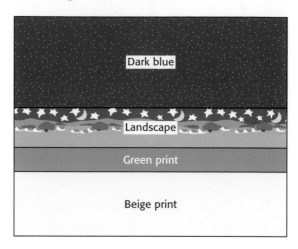

APPLIQUÉ

1. Following the directions in "Hand Appliqué" on
   page 9, trace each "Let Freedom Ring" pattern
   piece on pages 79–81 onto freezer paper. Using
   these freezer-paper templates, cut out each piece
   from your selected appliqué fabrics.

2. Following the quilt photograph on page 40 and
   the illustration on page 43, appliqué each piece in
   the following order:
   • 2 off-white rectangles, each 3" x 22"; appliqué
     them in place approximately 2½" from either
     edge of the quilt for porch posts.
   • Dress (A) from light floral print
   • Shirt (B) from plaid
   • Hands (C) from skin-tone fabric
   • Hat (D) and hat center (E) from light print
   • Man's head (F) from dark brown
   • 2 flower pots (G) from rust or dark red fabric
   • Rug (H) from light brown. Use a pin to fray the
     short edges of the piece to look like fringe.

BORDER

1. To attach the quilt border, refer to "Finishing the Quilt" on page 20. For an even border that lies flat, measure the length of the quilt through the center. From the navy blue border fabric, cut 2 strips, 4" wide by the quilt length measurement. Sew the strips to the sides of the quilt.

2. Measure the width of the quilt through the center, including the side border strips. From the navy blue border fabric, cut 1 strip, 4" wide by the quilt width measurement. Sew it to the bottom of the quilt.

3. From the banner or flag print, cut 1 strip, 6½" wide by the quilt width measurement. Sew this strip to the top of the quilt. Optional: If you're using a banner print, appliqué it to the top of the quilt, following the curved edges of the banner.

Border detail from "Let Freedom Ring"

Appliqué detail from "Let Freedom Ring"

FUSING THE FOURTH OF JULY MOTIFS

1. Referring to "Fusing" on page 10, cut out motifs from your theme fabric.

2. Referring to the quilt photograph on page 40, begin to fill your scene with motifs from your theme fabrics. Use the following suggestions as a guide:
   - Cut out flowers or strawberries for the flowerpots on the porch.
   - Place leaves along the columns of the front porch.
   - Add patriotic motifs to the rug.
   - Add a small flag motif to the lady's hand.
   - Use stars, Uncle Sam, and any other motifs from your fabrics to decorate the border. (Remember to search your computer graphic and clip-art programs for patriotic motifs, too.)

3. Continue to add motifs from your fabrics to fill the design. Pin all of the motifs in place.

4. When you are pleased with the arrangement of the motifs and the design of your quilt, fuse all the motifs in place with a hot iron.

EMBROIDERING THE MOTIFS

Refer to the directions in "Embroidering Motifs" on page 10, and use the color photograph as a placement guide for all embroidery accents. Blanket stitch around all of the fused motifs. Remember to change colors and use different types of thread as you embroider the various motifs.

EMBELLISHING YOUR DESIGN

1. Referring to the "Embellishing with Embroidery" on page 11 and "Additional Embellishments" on page 12, have fun adding details to your quilt. To begin, use a small (4" x 6") American flag to decorate one of the columns of the front porch. Make several folds in the flag and pin it in place on the quilt, referring to the photograph for placement. Blanket stitch or appliqué it to the quilt. Use an outline stitch to create a flagpole.

2. Add buttons such as small flags and stars to the borders of the quilt.

3. Using the beading pattern on page 82 as a guide, bead the lines of the fireworks with seed beads, bugle beads, or a combination. To sew beads in place, follow the directions in "Beaded Fringe and Beaded Lettering" on page 17.

4. Using the pattern on page 45, trace the words "Let Freedom Ring" to the bottom border of your quilt. (You can also write the words if you wish.) Using white seed beads, Nymo thread, and a size 10 quilting needle, attach seed beads along the marked lines.

5. After quilting and binding your project, remember to sign and date your work of art!

Flag detail from "Let Freedom Ring"

Beaded lettering detail from "Let Freedom Ring"

Let Freedom Ring
Beading Pattern

HALLOWEEN HAPPENINGS

HALLOWEEN HAPPENINGS BY JOANNE GOLDSTEIN, 2000, CORAL SPRINGS, FLORIDA, 36" X 32½".

The days are getting shorter and there is a cool, crisp breeze in the air. Pumpkins are bursting off their vines, and an orange moon glows brightly in the dark evening sky. As ghosts and goblins make their way across town, there are reports of strange happenings from the haunted house. With so many Halloween theme fabrics to choose from, you can make your own version of "Halloween Happenings" as scary or whimsical as you wish.

MATERIALS

Note: All fabrics are 100 percent–cotton quilting fabrics unless otherwise specified. All measurements are based on 42"-wide fabrics.

⅝ yd. sky print for sky
¼ yd. green print for grass
¼ yd. dark green print for path
8" square scrap of bright orange fabric for moon
¼ yd. black print for haunted house
¼ yd. bright yellow fabric for windows and door
⅜ yd. solid black fabric for trees
½ yd. second black print for borders
1¼ yds. backing fabric
1 yd. low-loft batting
Freezer paper
1 yd. fusible web
8" embroidery hoop

THEME FABRICS

Note: Be sure to purchase enough fabric for several repeats of each motif.

Collect Halloween fabrics with designs that include pumpkins, jack-o'-lanterns, ghosts, witches, bats, black cats, and scarecrows. You can set the tone for your Halloween quilt by choosing motifs that are scary, silly, primitive, or realistic.

Fabric suggestions

EMBELLISHING SUPPLIES

Embroidery floss, perle cotton, rayon floss, metallic
    floss, variegated embroidery thread, or decorative
    threads of your choice in assorted colors
Halloween buttons and charms to add texture and
    dimension to your quilt
One black seed bead for spider
Green embroidery floss
Green silk ribbon
White seed beads for lettering, Nymo beading thread,
    and size 10 quilting needle for attaching beads

Embellishing suggestions

CUTTING FOR BACKGROUND

From the sky print, cut:
    1 rectangle, 28" x 19"
From the green print, cut:
    1 strip, 28" x 7"

PIECING THE BACKGROUND

Join the 28" x 19" sky-print piece and 28" x 7" green-
print piece together as shown to complete the simple
background piecing.

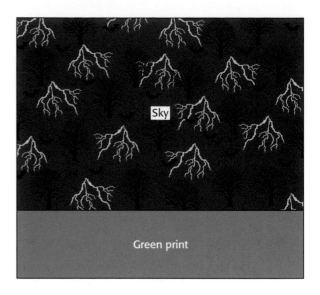

Sky

Green print

APPLIQUÉ

1. Following the directions in "Hand Appliqué" on
   page 9, trace each "Halloween Happenings" pattern
   piece on pages 83–88 onto freezer paper. Using
   these freezer-paper patterns, cut out each piece
   from your selected fabric.

2. Following the quilt photograph on page 46 and the
   illustration on page 49, appliqué each piece in
   place in the following order:
   • Path (A) from dark green print
   • Moon (B) from bright orange
   • Haunted house (C) from black print
   • Windows and door (D, E, F, G, and H) from
     bright yellow
   • 2 trees (I and I reverse) from solid black

FUSING THE HALLOWEEN MOTIFS

1. Referring to "Fusing" on page 10, cut out motifs from your theme fabric.

2. Referring to the quilt photograph on page 46, begin to place the motifs on the quilt top. Position ghost motifs coming out of a window and door on the house. Add a row of small pumpkins along the bottom of the house. To add depth and perspective to the design, position some larger pumpkins and jack-o'-lanterns towards the bottom of the quilt. Add some bats and owls in the trees and a witch flying in front of the moon. Let your theme fabric selection help you design the quilt. Try placing a black cat in the doorway of the house or a gravestone under the trees. A skeleton hanging from one of the tree branches or perhaps a witch's hat and broom near the house might work well. Use your imagination and continue to add motifs from your fabrics to fill the design. Pin all of the motifs in place.

3. Following the directions in "Padded Motifs" on page 15, choose several ghosts and pad them with batting for an extra dimensional effect.

4. When you are pleased with the arrangement of the motifs and the design of your quilt, fuse all the motifs in place with a hot iron.

EMBROIDERING THE MOTIFS

Refer to the directions in "Embroidering Motifs" on page 10, and use the color photograph as a placement guide for all embroidery accents. Blanket stitch around all of the fused motifs. Remember to use different colors and types of thread as you embroider the various motifs.

Embroidery detail from "Halloween Happenings"

EMBELLISHING YOUR DESIGN

1. Referring to "Embellishing with Embroidery" on page 11 and "Additional Embellishments" on page 12, have fun adding details to your quilt. To begin, use black perle cotton and the outline stitch to embroider a fence on each side of the path, referring to the quilt photograph for placement.

2. Referring to the illustration below, add a spider's web to one of the windows. Use 1 strand of embroidery floss to make 4 straight stitches about 1" long. Secure with a knot on the back of the quilt. Then come up at A and loop thread around the straight stitch at B, C, and D. Secure thread with a knot on the back. Repeat for each line of the web.

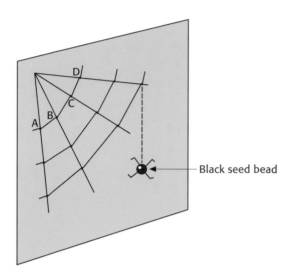

Black seed bead

3. Attach a spider to the web with a running stitch. Use a black seed bead for the spider's body and tiny straight stitches for its legs.

4. Use 2 strands of green embroidery floss to add stems to some of the pumpkins. Using silk ribbon and the leaf stitch, add a small leaf to each stem.

5. Place small pumpkin buttons on the fence to add texture to the quilt.

6. Referring to the directions for "Beaded Fringe and Beaded Lettering" on page 17, write or trace the word "BOO" from the pattern on page 86 onto the house; use the photograph as a placement guide. Use white seed beads, Nymo thread, and a size 10 quilting needle to attach the seed beads along the marked lines.

BORDER

1. To attach the border to the quilt, refer to "Finishing the Quilt" on page 20. For an even border that lies flat, measure the length of the quilt through the center. Cut 2 strips from the black-print border fabric, 4½" wide by quilt length measurement. Sew the border strips to the sides of the quilt.

2. Measure the width of the quilt through the center, including the side border strips. Cut 2 strips from the black-print border fabric, 4½" wide by the quilt width measurement. Sew the border strips to the top and bottom of the quilt.

3. Arrange additional motifs such as small ghosts, pumpkins, and jack-o'-lanterns along the lower border of the quilt. Fuse in place and embroider with the blanket stitch.

4. After quilting and binding your project, remember to sign and date your work of art!

Border detail from "Halloween Happenings"

BOUNTIFUL HARVEST

BOUNTIFUL HARVEST BY JOANNE GOLDSTEIN, 2000, CORAL SPRINGS, FLORIDA, 43" X 47".

Celebrate the Thanksgiving season and pay tribute to the gifts from a bountiful harvest by making this holiday collage quilt. This colorful wall hanging will be a festive addition to your holiday gathering. Theme fabrics are plentiful this time of year. Fabric shops are bursting with colorful, vibrant, and inspiring motifs to help you easily create a Thanksgiving collage. As you join your family and friends, let the fruits of the harvest grace your table and your home.

MATERIALS

Note: All fabrics are 100 percent–cotton quilting fabrics unless otherwise specified. All measurements are based on 42"-wide fabrics.

1 yd. solid black fabric for background
½ yd. black print for background
½ yd. subtle black print, such as a tone-on-tone or
    batik, for background
¼ yd. green print for stems
¼ yd. brown print for stems
½ yd. rust print for inner border and binding
¾ yd. fall print for wide border
1½ yds. backing fabric
1½ yds. low-loft batting
Freezer paper
1 yd. fusible web
8" embroidery hoop

THEME FABRICS

Note: Be sure to purchase enough fabric for several repeats of each motif.

Look for colorful motifs that will fill your design with a seasonal theme, such as autumn leaves and flowers, pumpkins, gourds, fruits, pinecones, and dried corn. If desired, add to your fabric motifs with the help of computer clip art.

Fabric suggestions

EMBELLISHING SUPPLIES

Embroidery floss, perle cotton, rayon floss, metallic
floss, variegated embroidery thread, or decorative
threads of your choice in assorted colors

1½ yds. gold metallic cord

Seed beads in assorted colors, Nymo beading thread,
and size 10 quilting needle for attaching beads

Decorative buttons and charms such as leaves, acorns,
pinecones, flowers, and pumpkins

Optional: polymer clay in yellow, green, and orange
for making accents such as flowers and leaves

Embellishing suggestions

CUTTING FOR BACKGROUND

From the solid black fabric, cut:

3 strips, 4½" x 42". Cut each strip into 4½" squares
for a total of 20 squares.

2 squares, 7" x 7". Cut each square in half diagonally
for a total of 4 corner triangles.

5 squares, 9" x 9". Cut each square twice diagonally
for a total of 20 side-setting triangles. (You'll
have 2 left over.)

From the black print, cut:

4 strips, 4½" x 42". Cut each strip into 4½" squares
for a total of 30 squares.

From the subtle black print, cut:

1 rectangle, 14" x 29"

PIECING THE BACKGROUND

Set the squares and triangles together in diagonal rows,
as shown in the illustration. Be sure to alternate the
solid black and black-print squares to create a subtle
checkerboard pattern.

Background piecing detail from "Bountiful Harvest"

APPLIQUÉ

1. Following the directions in "Hand Appliqué" on page 9, and referring to the illustration below, center the 14" x 29" subtle black-print rectangle over the pieced quilt top. Appliqué the rectangle in place.

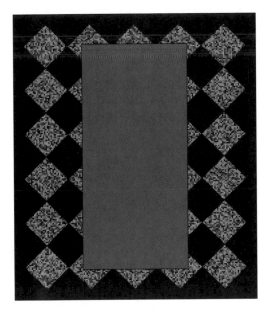

2. From the back of the quilt, carefully cut away the fabric behind the appliquéd rectangle to reduce any bulk.

Appliqué detail from "Bountiful Harvest"

FUSING THE THANKSGIVING MOTIFS

1. Referring to "Fusing" on page 10, cut out motifs from your theme fabric.

2. Referring to the quilt photograph on page 52, begin to place the motifs on the quilt top. Fill your scene with motifs from your theme fabrics to create an abundant harvest scene. Use the following suggestions as a guide:
   - Cut out and arrange the harvest vegetables, leaves, and flowers over the center panel of the pieced background.
   - Position some of the larger motifs in the center of the design.
   - Use an interesting assortment of harvest vegetables, autumn leaves and flowers, pumpkins, and gourds.
   - The motifs should be close together and overlap in several places (see photograph). Fill in empty areas of the design with leaf motifs.
   - Place several colorful leaves along the sides of the design.

3. Pin all of the motifs in place, but don't fuse the motifs until the stems made with bias strips are appliquéd in place.

4. Referring to the directions for "Bias Strips for Stems and More" on page 9, make approximately 5 green and 3 brown ¼"-wide bias strips for stems. Using the quilt photograph as a placement guide, pin the bias-strip stems in place, tucking them under some of the motifs. Wind the stems through the design so that some of the motifs seem to be attached to the stems.

5. To suggest delicate stems and tendrils and to add sparkle to the design, wind and loop gold metallic cord over and under some of the bias-strip stems Using metallic thread and a tiny straight stitch, couch all of the metallic cord. Space the couching stitches so that they secure all of the loops.

6. Appliqué all of the stems in place.

7. Place several of the vegetable and leaf motifs along the stems. When you are pleased with the arrangement of the motifs and your quilt design, fuse all the motifs in place.

Motif detail from "Bountiful Harvest"

EMBROIDERING THE MOTIFS

Refer to the directions in "Embroidering Motifs" on page 10 and use the color photograph as a placement guide for all embroidery accents. Blanket stitch around all of the fused motifs. Remember to change colors and to use different types of thread as you embroider the various fruits, vegetables, and leaves.

EMBELLISHING YOUR DESIGN

1. Referring to "Embellishing with Embroidery" on page 11 and "Additional Embellishments" on page 12, have fun adding details to your quilt. To begin, use green silk ribbon and the Japanese ribbon stitch to add leaves to some of the bias-strip stems.

2. Use the featherstitch and 2 strands of thread to indicate sprays of foliage and to fill in sparse areas in the design.

3. Add seed beads to the center of some of the flowers for highlights. You can add seed beads on top of some of the vegetables to highlight them, too.

4. Attach buttons such as leaves and flowers to some of the bias-strip stems to add texture and dimension to your collage. Or, you can make your own accents using polymer clay (see page 18).

BORDERS

1. To attach the borders to the quilt, refer to "Finishing the Quilt" on page 20. For even borders that lie flat, measure the length of the quilt through the center. Cut 2 strips from the rust-print inner border fabric, 2" wide by the quilt length measurement. Sew the border strips to the sides of the quilt.

2. Measure the width of the quilt through the center, including the side border strips. Cut 2 more strips from the rust-print fabric, 2" wide by the quilt width measurement. Sew the border strips to the top and bottom of your quilt.

3. To make the wide outer border, repeat steps 1 and 2 with the fall-print border fabric; cut each strip 4½" wide. Measure your quilt through the center to determine the width and length measurements.

4. After quilting and binding your project, remember to sign and date your work of art!

Border detail from "Bountiful Harvest"

CHRISTMAS IS IN THE AIR

CHRISTMAS IS IN THE AIR BY JOANNE GOLDSTEIN, 2000, CORAL SPRINGS, FLORIDA, 27" x 27".

As the excitement of the holiday season approaches, we all begin to "feather our nest" with our traditional adornments. This fun-to-make wintry wall hanging celebrates the holiday season with cardinals, poinsettias, holly leaves, and bells. Let your theme fabric choices help you to design your own version of "Christmas Is in the Air."

MATERIALS

Note: All fabrics are 100 percent–cotton quilting fabrics unless otherwise specified. All measurements are based on 42"-wide fabrics.

½ yd. light blue fabric for background
1 yd. medium blue fabric for background and binding
⅜ yd. green fabric for birdhouse
¼ yd. white fabric for roof and birdhouse base
⅛ yd. reddish brown fabric for chimney
Scrap of gold fabric (cotton or lamé) for star
¼ yd. brown fabric for wooden post and hole
½ yd. dark green fabric for branches
1 yd. fabric for backing
1 yd. batting
Freezer paper
1 yd. fusible web
8" embroidery hoop

THEME FABRICS

Note: Be sure to purchase enough fabric for several repeats of each motif.

Buy enough bird-print fabric(s) so you'll have 2 or 3 full birds. You'll also need about 12 large and 6 small flowers cut from Christmas prints with poinsettias, holly, or other seasonal flowers. Finally, cut 2 bells, 5 to 7 pinecones, and a ribbon and bow motif from theme fabric.

Fabric suggestions

EMBELLISHING SUPPLIES

Embroidery floss, perle cotton, rayon floss, metallic floss, variegated embroidery thread, or decorative threads of your choice in assorted colors

Seed beads in assorted colors, Nymo beading thread, and size 10 quilting needle for attaching beads

1 yd. string of red beads

Decorative buttons and charms such bells, stars, holly, and berries

Embellishing suggestions

CUTTING FOR BACKGROUND

From *each* of the light blue and medium blue background fabrics, cut:

6 strips, 2" x 42"

From the remaining medium blue fabric, cut:

3 strips, 5" x 42". Cut each strip into 5" squares for a total of 18 squares.

PIECING THE BACKGROUND

1. Join the light and medium blue 2" x 42" strips as shown to make 2 of Strip Set A and 2 of Strip Set B. For Strip Set A, sew 2 medium blue strips on either side of a center light blue strip. For Strip Set B, reverse the colors so that the medium blue strip is in the center. Your strip sets should measure 5" wide when complete. Press all seams toward the medium blue strips.

2. Cut each strip set into 2"-wide segments as shown.

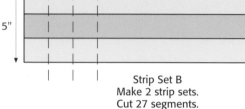

Strip Set A
Make 2 strip sets.
Cut 27 segments.

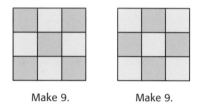

Strip Set B
Make 2 strip sets.
Cut 27 segments.

3. Join the segments together to make Nine Patch blocks as shown.

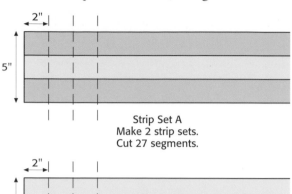

Make 9.   Make 9.

4. Alternately stitch the Nine Patch blocks and 5" medium blue squares together into rows. Join the rows together to complete the pieced background as shown.

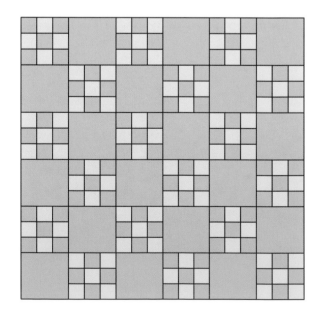

APPLIQUÉ

1. Following the directions in "Hand Appliqué" on page 9, trace each "Christmas Is in the Air" pattern piece on pages 89–92 onto freezer paper. Using these freezer-paper templates, cut out each piece from your selected fabric.

2. Following the quilt photograph on page 58 and the illustration below, appliqué each piece in place in the following order:
   - Birdhouse (A and B) from green fabric
   - Roof (C and D) from white fabric
   - Chimney (E) from reddish brown fabric
   - Snow on chimney (F) from white fabric
   - Star (G) from gold fabric
   - Wooden post (9" x 7" rectangle) from brown fabric
   - Birdhouse base (H) from white fabric
   - Hole (I) from brown fabric

3. Following the directions for making "Bias Strips for Stems and More" on page 9, make five ¼"-wide bias-strip branches from the dark green fabric. Appliqué the bias-strip branches in place by using the photograph on page 58 and the illustration below as placement guides.

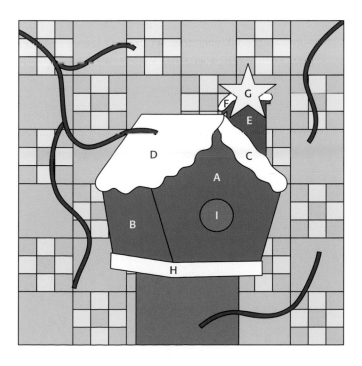

Appliqué detail from "Christmas Is in the Air"

Appliqué detail from "Christmas Is in the Air"

FUSING THE CHRISTMAS MOTIFS

1. Referring to "Fusing" on page 10, cut out motifs from your theme fabric.

2. Referring to the quilt photograph on page 58, begin to place the motifs on the quilt top. Place poinsettias, holly leaves, and pinecones along the bias-strip branches. To add depth and perspective to the design, allow some of the flowers to overlap and move off the edges of the quilt. Tuck ribbon motifs under some of the foliage. Place cardinals or other colorful winter birds on the birdhouse roof and base and on one of the branches. Add bells and holly leaves to the front of the birdhouse. Place several sprays of holly leaves on both sides of the roof, the base, and on the front of the wooden post. Continue to add motifs from your fabrics to fill the design. Pin all of the motifs in place.

3. When you are pleased with the arrangement of all the motifs and your quilt design, fuse all the motifs in place with a hot iron.

4. Referring to the directions in "Dimensional Motifs" on page 14, cut out extra poinsettias to make some of the flowers look dimensional. Don't attach these motifs to the quilt top yet.

EMBROIDERING THE MOTIFS

Refer to the directions in "Embroidering Motifs" on page 10 and use the quilt photograph as a placement guide for all embroidery accents. Blanket stitch around all of the fused motifs. Remember to change colors and use different types of thread as you embroider the various motifs.

EMBELLISHING YOUR DESIGN

1. Referring to "Embellishing with Embroidery" on page 11 and "Additional Embellishments" on page 12, have fun adding details to your quilt. To begin, use the outline stitch to indicate pine needles along the bias-strip branches.

2. Stitch white seed beads along the pine needles for snow.

3. Add beads to the center of the flowers for highlight and interest. Place the extra poinsettias that you prepared for dimensional interest over the fused poinsettia motifs and anchor their centers with beads. The petals remain free of the quilt to add dimension to your collage.

4. Sew the string of red beads to the birdhouse roof and base to indicate holiday trim.

5. Add small red beads or buttons to the center of each cluster of holly leaves.

6. Attach tiny, gold, star buttons to the center of the ribbon ornaments on the birdhouse and the wooden post.

7. To add texture to the quilt, use small buttons such as holly leaves, pinecones, and flowers.

8. After quilting and binding your project, remember to sign and date your work of art!

Beading detail from "Christmas Is in the Air"

FESTIVAL OF LIGHTS BY JOANNE GOLDSTEIN, 2000, CORAL SPRINGS, FLORIDA, 36½" X 29½".

Celebrate the Festival of Lights with a holiday collage quilt honoring the symbols of the Hanukkah season. Adorn your quilt with motifs such as menorahs, the Star of David, dreidels, the Torah, and gold coins. In the quilt shown on page 64, the menorah sits in front of a window with crazy-pieced panes that encorporate many traditional holiday motifs. Make this Hanukkah collage quilt and it will become part of your own holiday traditions.

MATERIALS

Note: All fabrics are 100 percent-cotton quilting fabrics unless otherwise specified. All measurements are based on 42"-wide fabrics.

¼ yd. each of 5–8 different blue prints for window

¼ yd. gold print for sashing

5" x 12" (approximately) rectangle cut from a lace doily, place mat, or table runner

¾ yd. gold fabric for border

¼ yd. gold fabric (cotton or lamé) for menorah

Scraps of bright orange fabric for candle flames

8" square of light print for vase

¼ yd. blue fabric for bias strips

1 yd. backing fabric

½ yd. binding fabric

1 yd. low-loft batting

Freezer paper

1 yd. fusible web

8" embroidery hoop

THEME FABRICS

Note: Measurements are approximate; be sure to purchase enough fabric for several repeats of each motif.

You'll need approximately ½ yard of Hanukkah holiday fabrics. Look for fabrics with large motifs that are easy to cut out and include dreidels, the Star of David, gold coins, menorahs, and the Torah. If desired, add to your fabric motifs with computer clip art.

You'll also need about ½ yard of a colorful floral fabric (or fabrics) for the flower arrangement in the vase.

Fabric suggestions

EMBELLISHING SUPPLIES

Embroidery floss, perle cotton, rayon floss, metallic
floss, variegated embroidery thread, or decorative
threads of your choice in assorted colors. Gold and
silver metallic threads and flosses give lots of
sparkle and highlights to the holiday motifs.

Seed beads in assorted colors, Nymo beading thread,
and size 10 quilting needle to attach beads

Gold bugle beads for highlights in the flames

Buttons and charms such as gold coins and the Star
of David

Embellishing suggestions

CUTTING FOR BACKGROUND

1. From the blue prints, cut a total of twelve 8"
   squares. Make sure not to cut more than 3 squares
   from the same blue print.

2. Stack 4 different blue squares on top of each other
   in a neat pile. Make 2 more piles, each with 4
   different blue squares.

3. Using the cutting diagram below and following the
   numerical order, slash the first stack along each
   cutting line. It is not necessary to mark each line.
   Simply use your rotary cutter to make 3 slashes.
   Be sure to cut the entire stack at once to ensure
   that the size and shape of the pieces are the same.

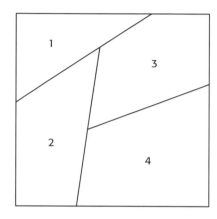

4. Repeat with the remaining 2 stacks of blocks
   until all of the blocks have been cut. Keep each
   stack separate.

5. From the gold-print sashing fabric, cut four 1¼" x
   42" strips. From 2 of the strips, cut a total of nine
   1¼" x 6½" segments.

PIECING THE BACKGROUND

1. Starting with 1 stack of cut squares, rearrange the
   pieces so that each square is composed of 4 different fabrics. To make the first of 4 pieced blocks,
   sew the 4 different fabric pieces together in the
   reverse order that they were cut in step 1 of
   "Cutting for Background." Sew piece 4 to piece 3
   to make a unit, and press the seam. Then sew the
   unit to piece 2; press. Finally, sew the unit to piece
   1 to complete 1 pieced block.

2. Repeat step 1 to make the remaining 3 pieced blocks from the first stack of cut squares. Then repeat the process for the other 2 stacks of cut squares.

3. Trim each pieced block into a 6½" x 6½" square. You will have a total of 12 pieced blocks.

4. Join the pieced squares and 6½" sashing strips together into 3 rows as shown.

5. Measure the width of your 3 completed rows. (If they are different lengths, take the average of the 3 measurements.) Trim the two 1¼" x 42" gold-print sashing strips to this measurement.

6. Join the rows together with long sashing strips separating the rows of pieced squares and short sashing strips.

7. Place the 5" x 12" rectangle from a lace doily, place mat, or table runner on the quilt top; use the photograph as a placement guide. Baste the raw or cut edge of the doily to the lower edge of the pieced quilt top.

BORDER

1. To attach the border to the quilt, refer to "Finishing the Quilt" on page 20. For an even border that lies flat, measure the length of the pieced quilt through the center. Cut 2 strips from the gold border fabric, 6½" wide by the quilt length measurement. Sew the border strips to the sides of the quilt.

2. Measure the width of the quilt through the center, including the side border strips. Cut 2 strips, 6½" wide by the quilt width measurement. Sew the border strips to the top and bottom of the quilt.

APPLIQUÉ

1. Following the directions in "Hand Appliqué" on page 9, trace each "Festival of Lights" pattern piece on pages 93–94 onto freezer paper. Using these freezer-paper templates, cut out each piece from your selected appliqué fabric.

2. Flip the lace doily down over the border and appliqué the edges in place.

3. Following the photograph on page 64, appliqué each piece in place in the following order:
   • Menorah (A–E) from gold cotton or lamé. Menorah should be centered over the lace doily.
   • Flames (F) from bright orange fabric (9 total)
   • Vase (G) from light print

4. Referring to the directions in "Bias Strips for Stems and More" on page 9, make two ¼" bias strips, each 10" long, from blue fabric for bias strips. Position 1 bias strip on each of the lower corners of the border. Appliqué in place.

FUSING THE HANUKKAH MOTIFS

1. Referring to "Fusing" on page 10, cut out motifs from your theme fabric.

2. Referring to the quilt photograph on page 64, begin to place the motifs on the quilt top. Place motifs such as dreidels and the Star of David into some of the crazy-pieced sections of the background.

3. Cut out and arrange several colorful flowers in the vase. Place them close together and position them so that several of the motifs overlap.

4. Choose a large Star of David and place it over the center of the menorah for decoration. Similarly, place a smaller motif in the center of the vase.

5. Cut out several large dreidels to place next to the menorah and vase of flowers.

6. Add motifs from your fabrics to the bias strips in the corners of the quilt.

7. If desired, use dimensional appliqué for one or more of the tabletop dreidels, referring to the directions in "Dimensional Motifs" on page 14 and "Layering" on page 15.

8. Continue to add motifs from your fabrics to fill the design. Pin all of the motifs in place. When you are pleased with the arrangement of all the motifs and the design of your quilt, fuse all the motifs in place with a hot iron.

EMBROIDERING THE MOTIFS

Refer to the directions in "Embroidering Motifs" on page 10 and use the color photograph as a placement guide for all embroidery accents. Blanket stitch around all of the fused motifs. Remember to change colors and use different types of thread as you embroider the various motifs.

EMBELLISHING YOUR DESIGN

1. Referring to "Embellishing with Embroidery" on page 11 and "Additional Embellishments" on page 12, have fun adding details to your quilt. To begin, use the stem stitch to anchor some of the flowers in the vase.

2. Use seed beads to highlight the centers of the flowers.

3. Use three gold bugle beads in the center of each candle flame to add sparkle.

4. If desired, add gold coin charms or buttons next to the dreidels to add texture and dimensional interest to the collage.

5. After quilting and binding your project, remember to sign and date your work of art!

·: PATTERNS ·~

Appliqué detail from "For Mother"

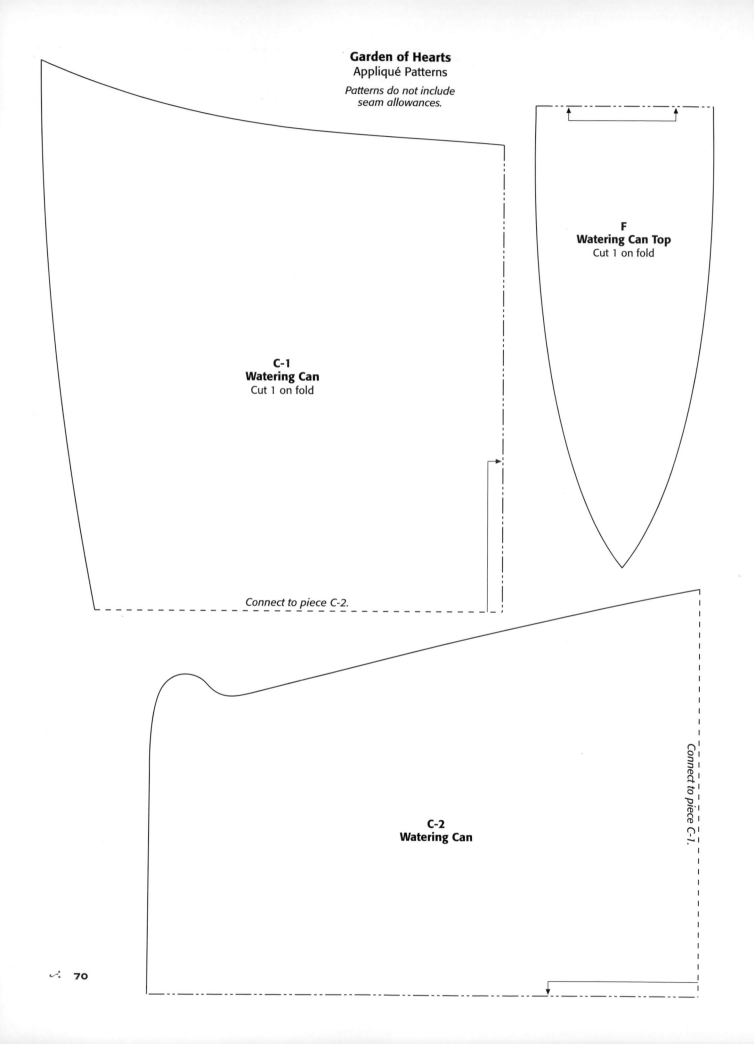

Garden of Hearts
Appliqué Patterns

*Patterns do not include
seam allowances.*

**F
Watering Can Top**
Cut 1 on fold

**C-1
Watering Can**
Cut 1 on fold

Connect to piece C-2.

Connect to piece C-1.

**C-2
Watering Can**

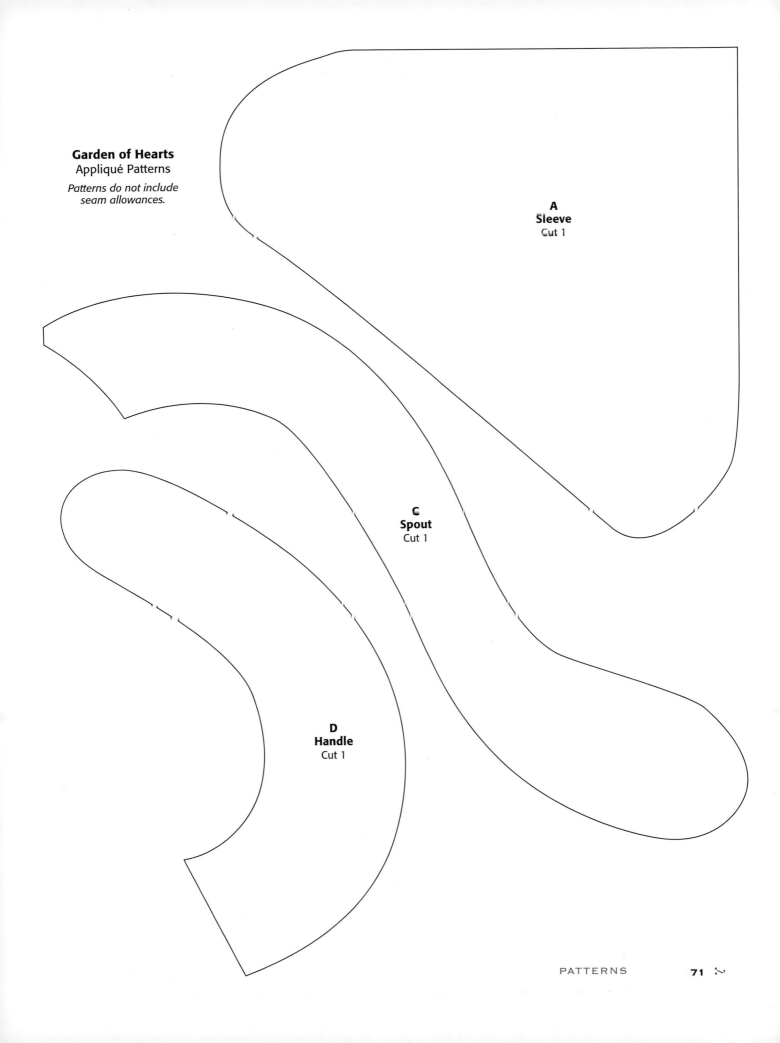

Garden of Hearts
Appliqué Patterns

*Patterns do not include
seam allowances.*

A
Sleeve
Cut 1

C
Spout
Cut 1

D
Handle
Cut 1

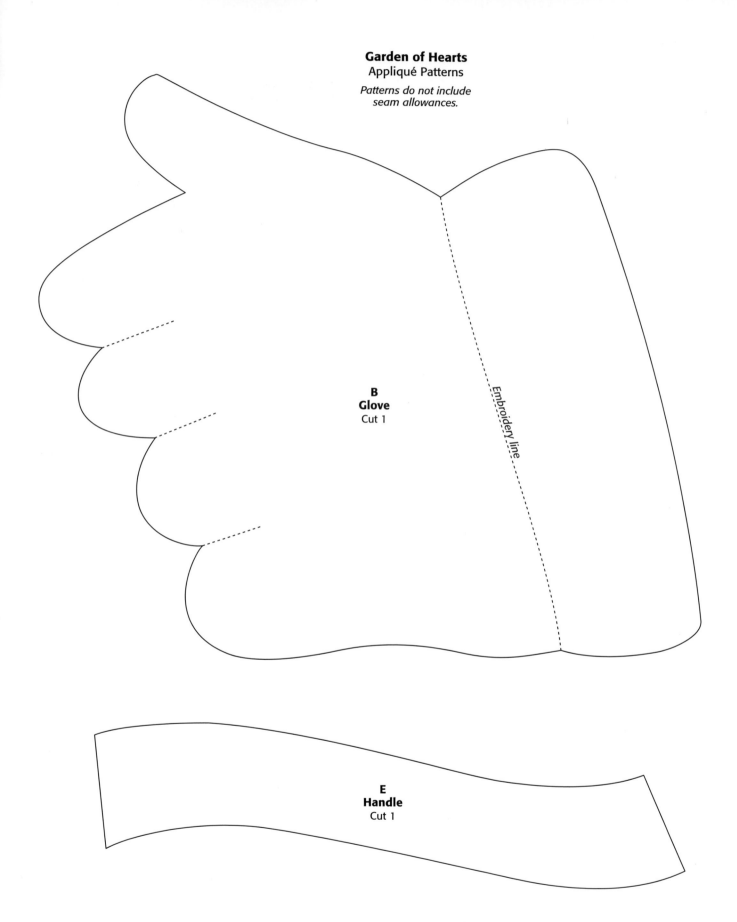

Garden of Hearts
Appliqué Patterns

*Patterns do not include
seam allowances.*

**B
Glove**
Cut 1

Embroidery line

**E
Handle**
Cut 1

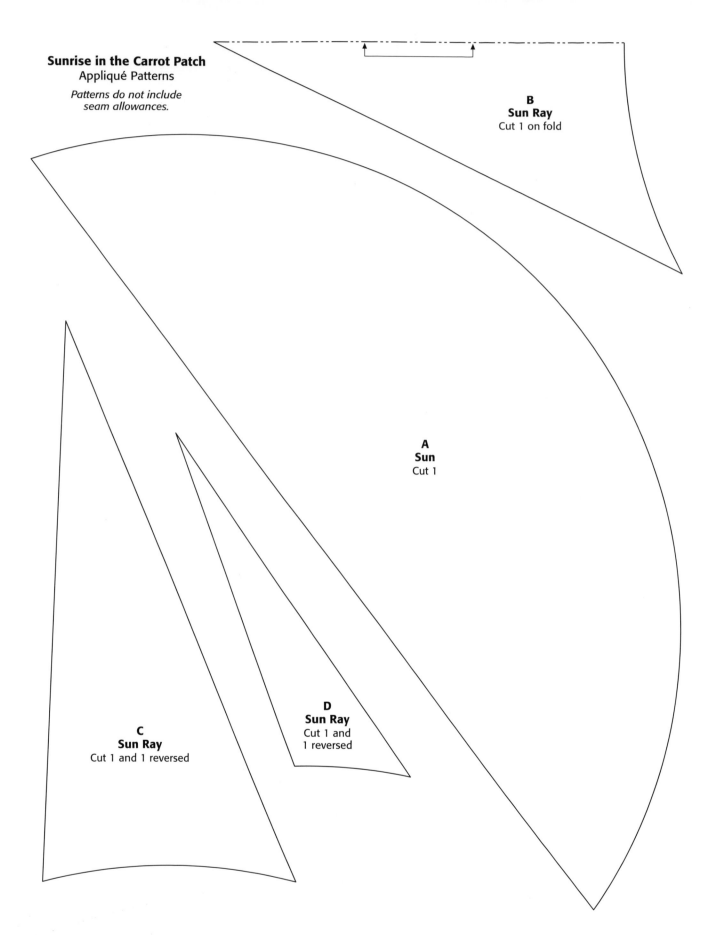

Sunrise in the Carrot Patch
Appliqué Patterns

Patterns do not include seam allowances.

B
Sun Ray
Cut 1 on fold

A
Sun
Cut 1

C
Sun Ray
Cut 1 and 1 reversed

D
Sun Ray
Cut 1 and
1 reversed

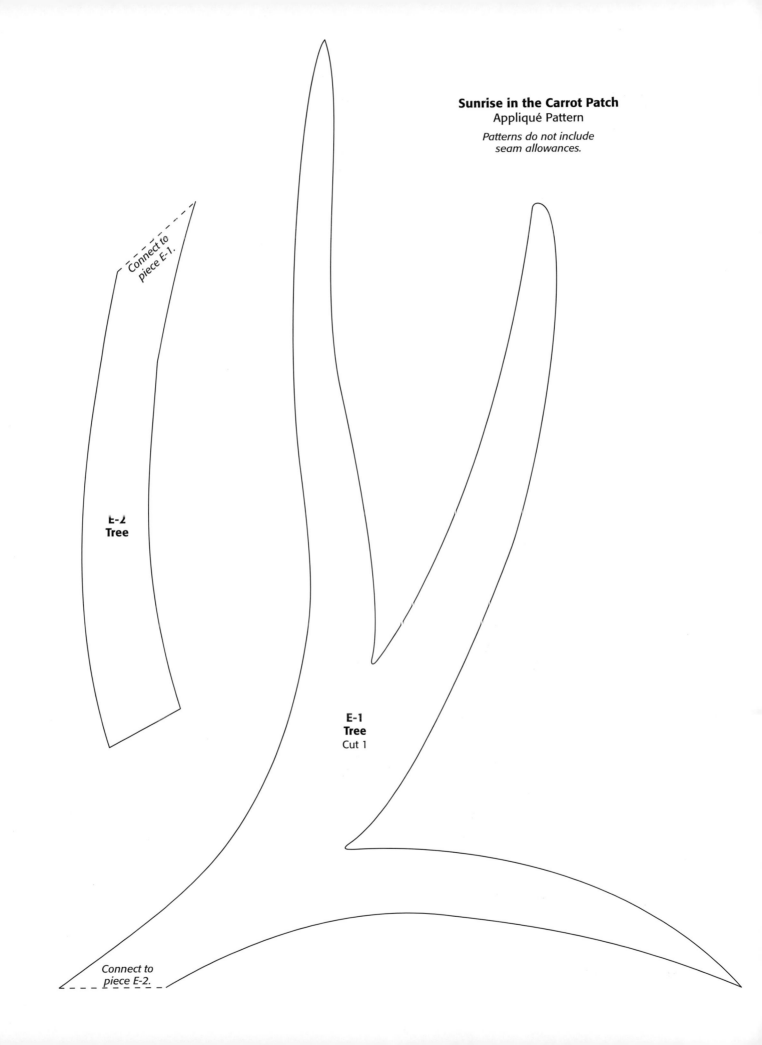

Sunrise in the Carrot Patch
Appliqué Pattern

*Patterns do not include
seam allowances.*

Connect to
piece E-1.

E-2
Tree

E-1
Tree
Cut 1

Connect to
piece E-2.

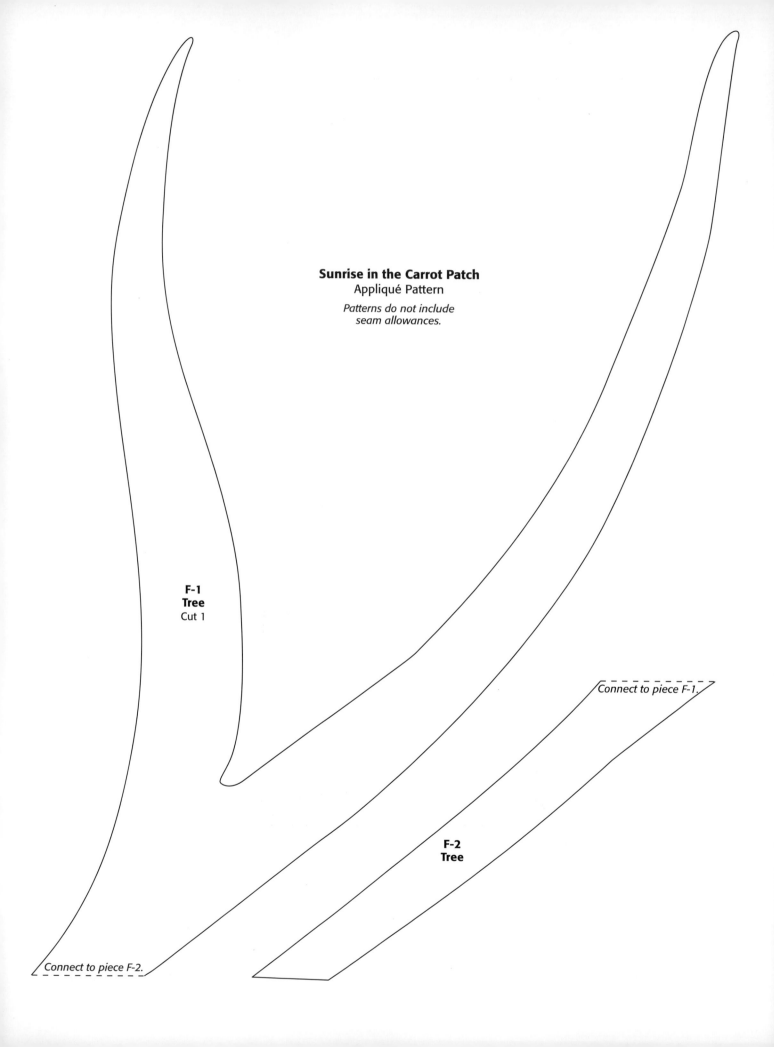

Sunrise in the Carrot Patch
Appliqué Pattern

*Patterns do not include
seam allowances.*

**F-1
Tree**
Cut 1

Connect to piece F-1.

**F-2
Tree**

Connect to piece F-2.

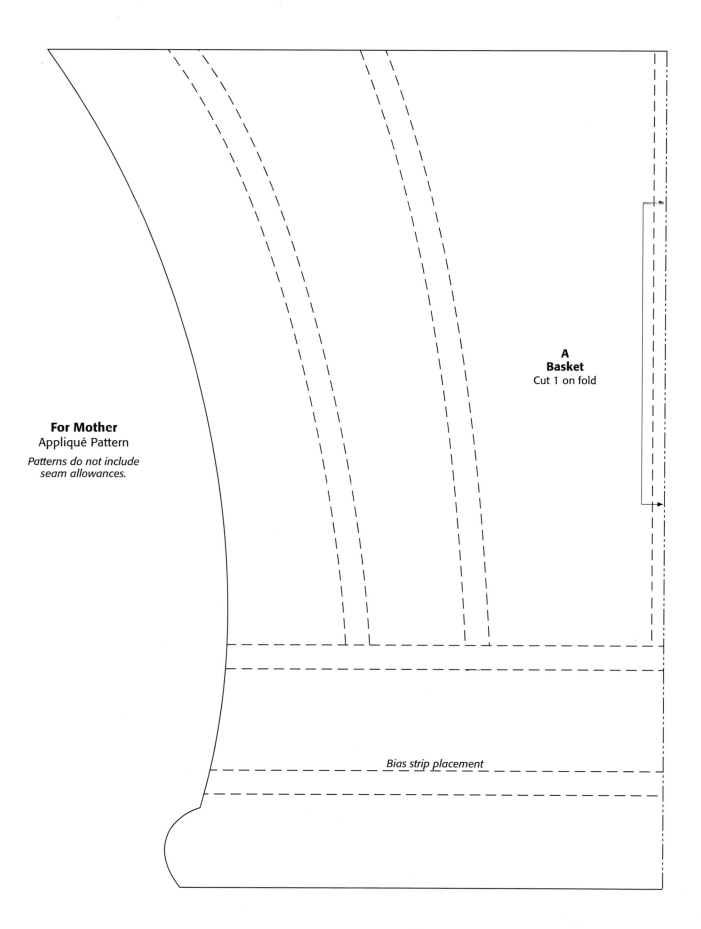

For Mother
Appliqué Pattern

Patterns do not include seam allowances.

A
Basket
Cut 1 on fold

Bias strip placement

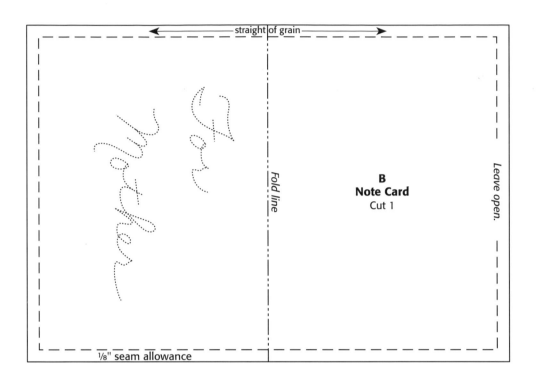

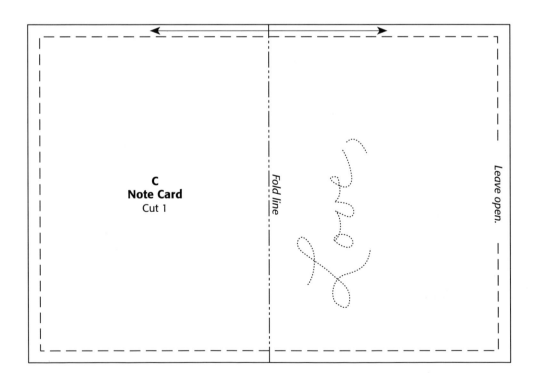

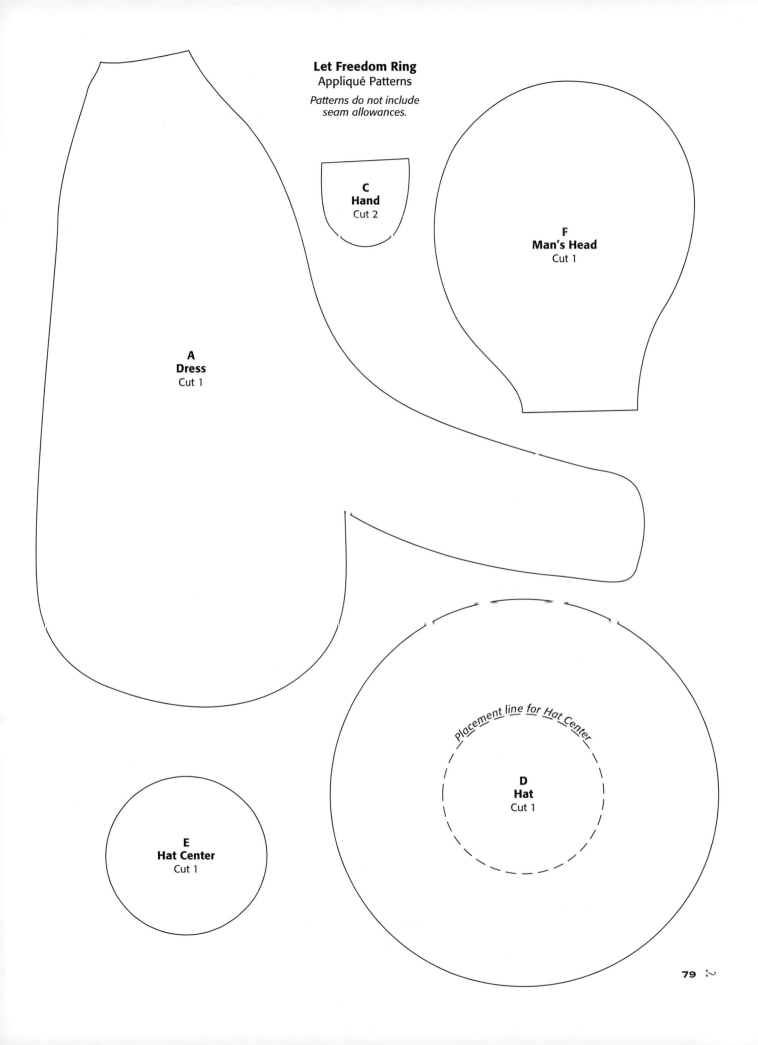

Let Freedom Ring
Appliqué Patterns

*Patterns do not include
seam allowances.*

C
Hand
Cut 2

F
Man's Head
Cut 1

A
Dress
Cut 1

D
Hat
Cut 1

Placement line for Hat Center

E
Hat Center
Cut 1

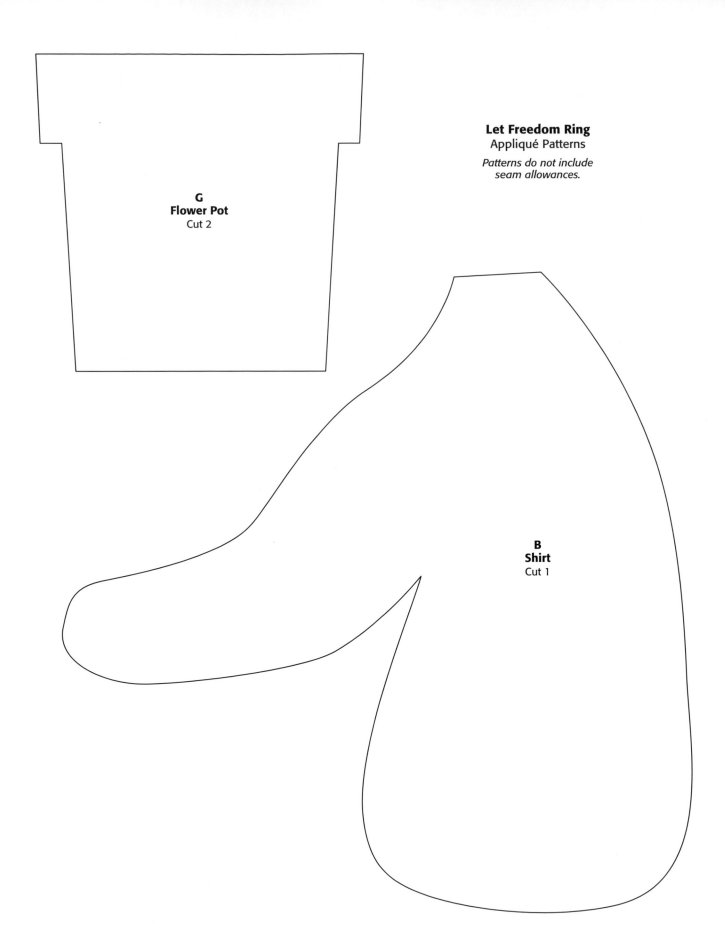

G
Flower Pot
Cut 2

Let Freedom Ring
Appliqué Patterns

Patterns do not include
seam allowances.

B
Shirt
Cut 1

Let Freedom Ring
Appliqué Pattern

*Patterns do not include
seam allowances.*

H
Rug
Cut 1

Let Freedom Ring
Beading Pattern

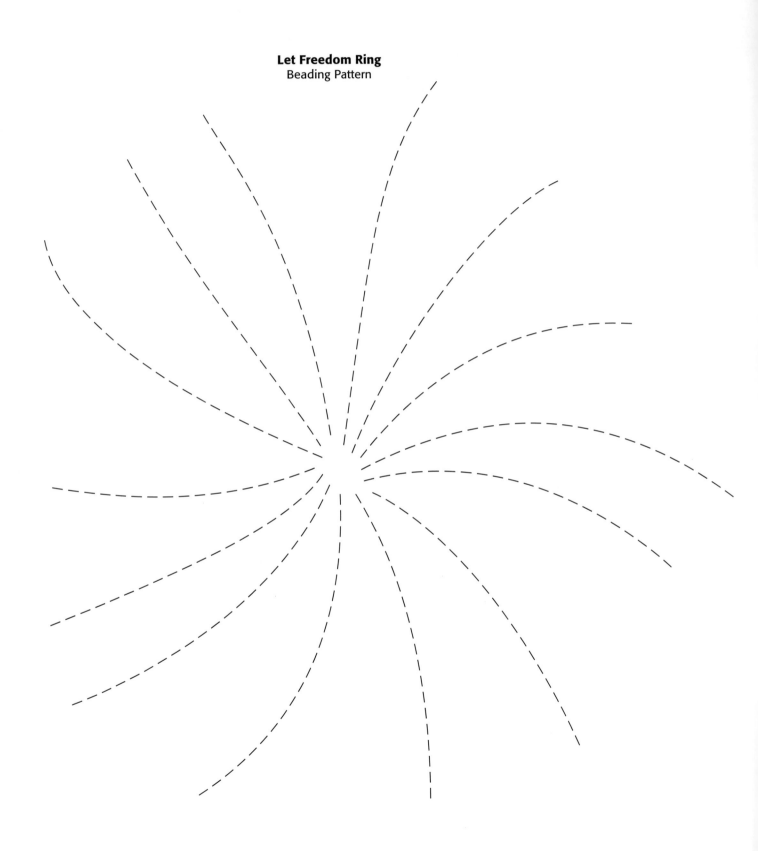

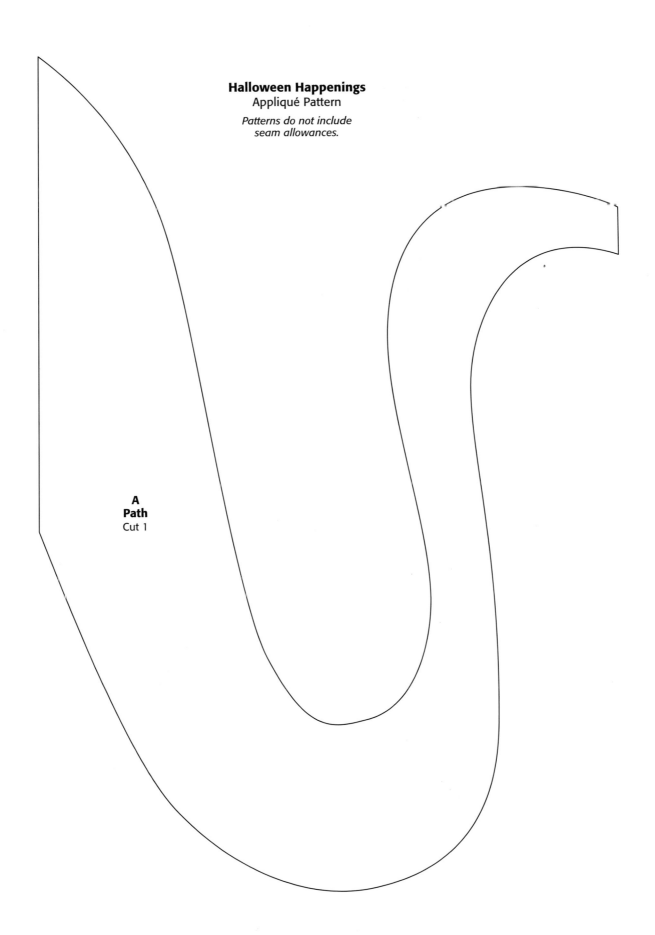

Halloween Happenings
Appliqué Pattern

*Patterns do not include
seam allowances.*

A
Path
Cut 1

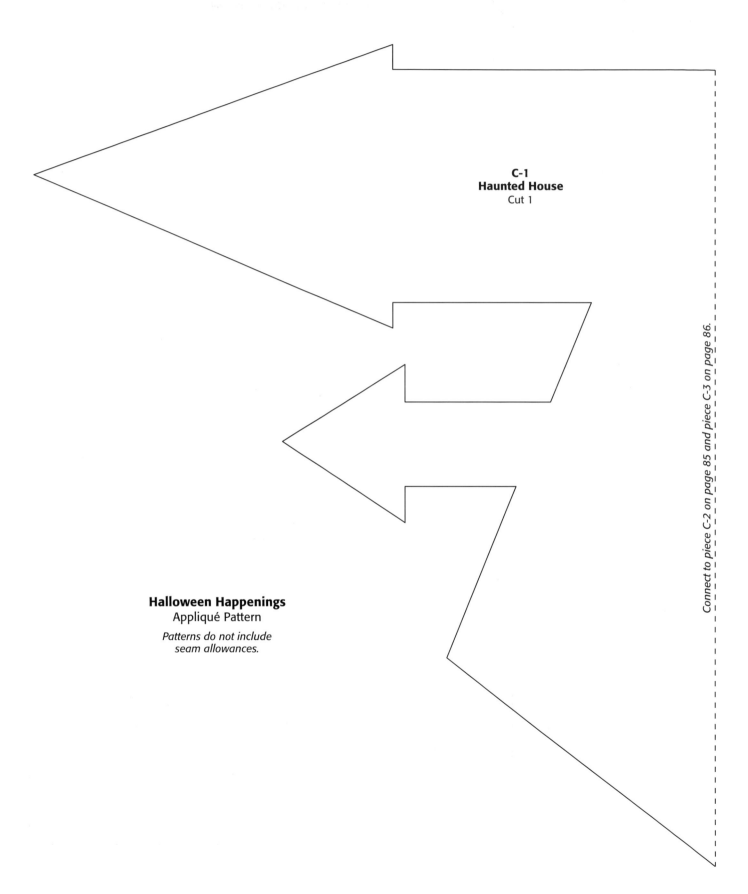

C-1
Haunted House
Cut 1

Halloween Happenings
Appliqué Pattern

*Patterns do not include
seam allowances.*

Connect to piece C-2 on page 85 and piece C-3 on page 86.

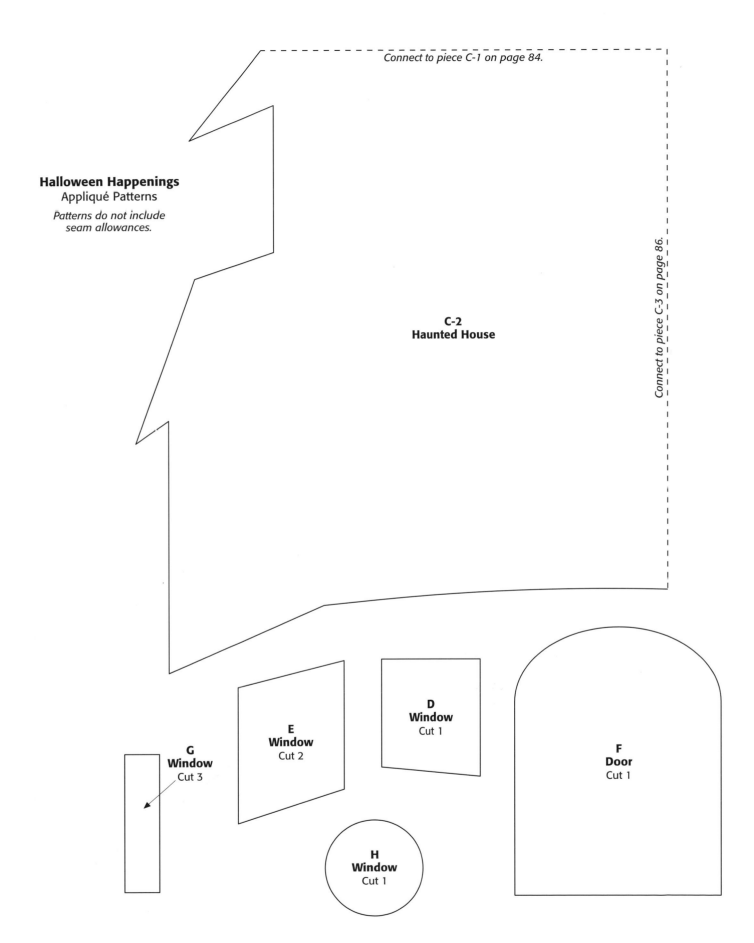

Halloween Happenings
Appliqué Patterns

*Patterns do not include
seam allowances.*

Connect to piece C-1 on page 84.

Connect to piece C-3 on page 86.

**C-2
Haunted House**

**G
Window**
Cut 3

**E
Window**
Cut 2

**D
Window**
Cut 1

**F
Door**
Cut 1

**H
Window**
Cut 1

Halloween Happenings
Appliqué and Beading Patterns

*Patterns do not include
seam allowances.*

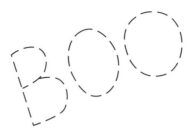

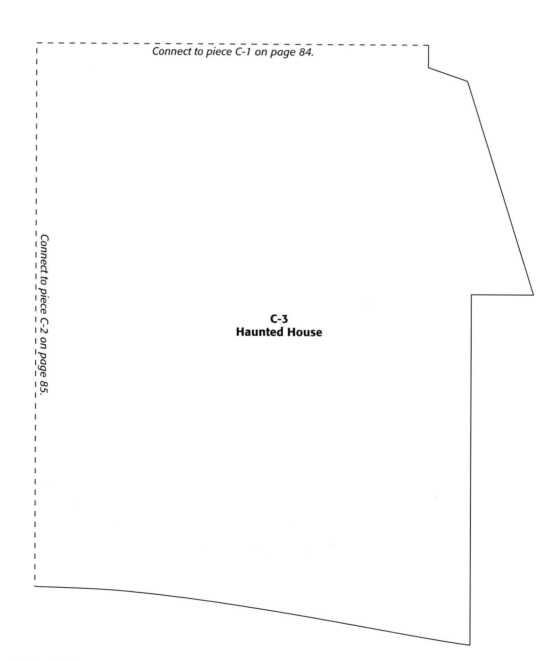

Connect to piece C-1 on page 84.

Connect to piece C-2 on page 85.

**C-3
Haunted House**

Halloween Happenings
Appliqué Pattern

*Patterns do not include
seam allowances.*

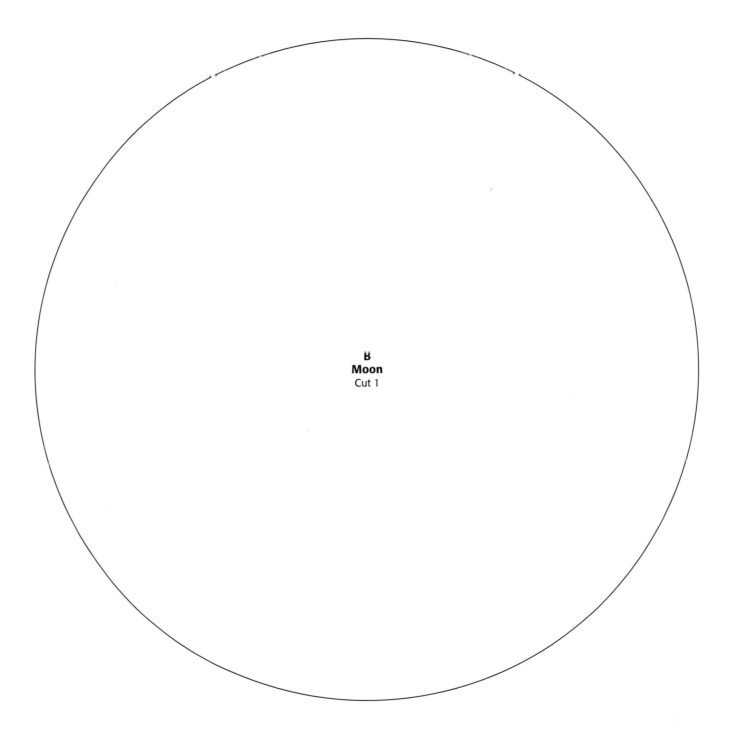

B
Moon
Cut 1

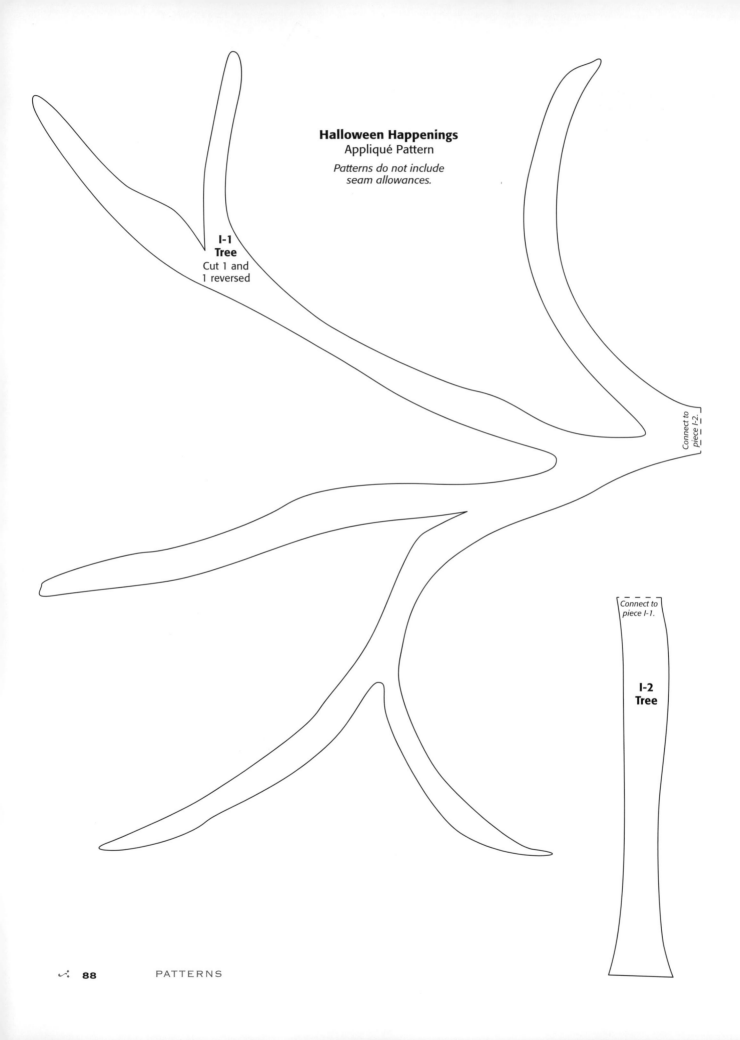

Halloween Happenings
Appliqué Pattern

*Patterns do not include
seam allowances.*

**I-1
Tree**
Cut 1 and
1 reversed

*Connect to
piece I-2.*

*Connect to
piece I-1.*

**I-2
Tree**

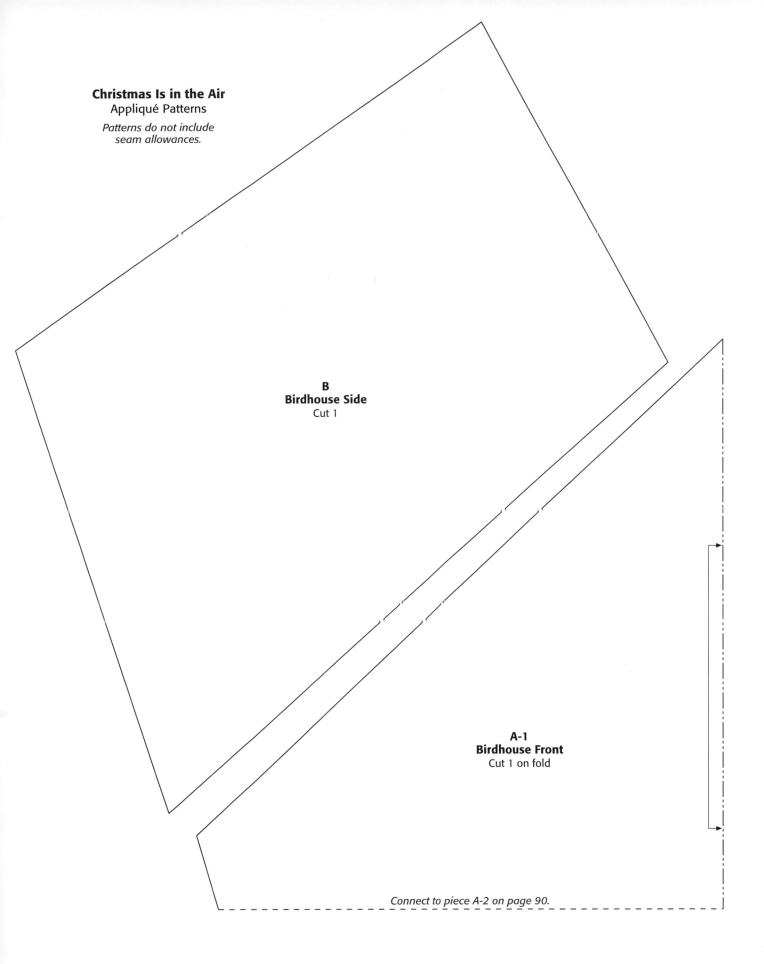

Christmas Is in the Air
Appliqué Patterns

*Patterns do not include
seam allowances.*

B
Birdhouse Side
Cut 1

A-1
Birdhouse Front
Cut 1 on fold

Connect to piece A-2 on page 90.

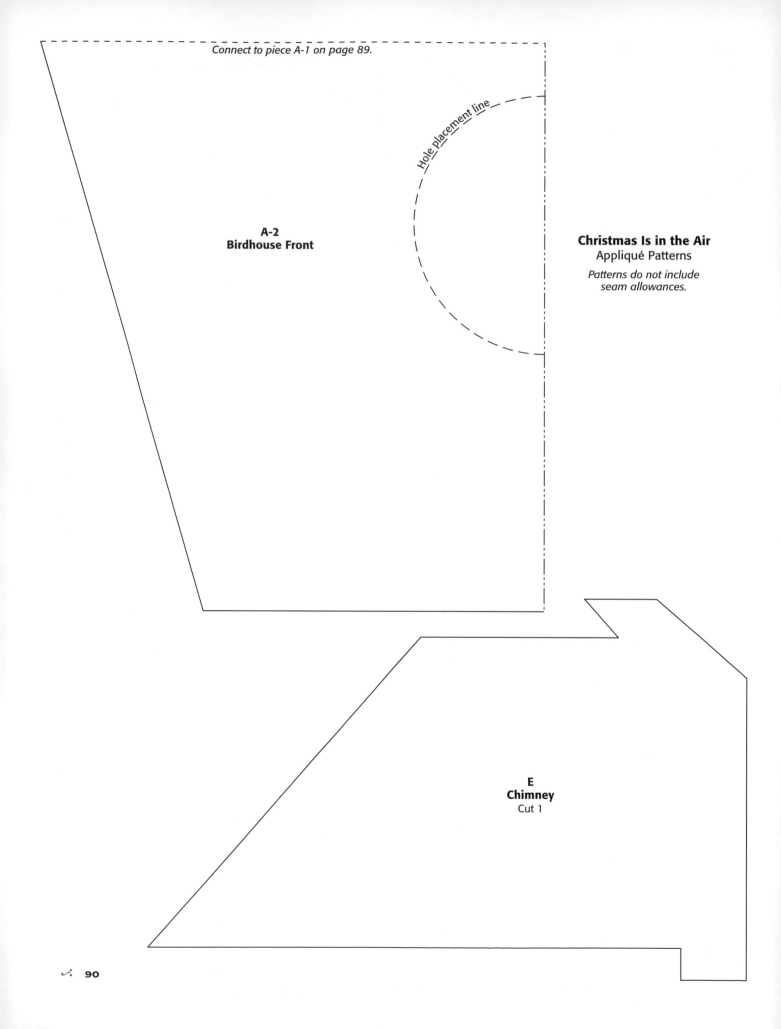

Connect to piece A-1 on page 89.

Hole placement line

A-2
Birdhouse Front

Christmas Is in the Air
Appliqué Patterns

*Patterns do not include
seam allowances.*

E
Chimney
Cut 1

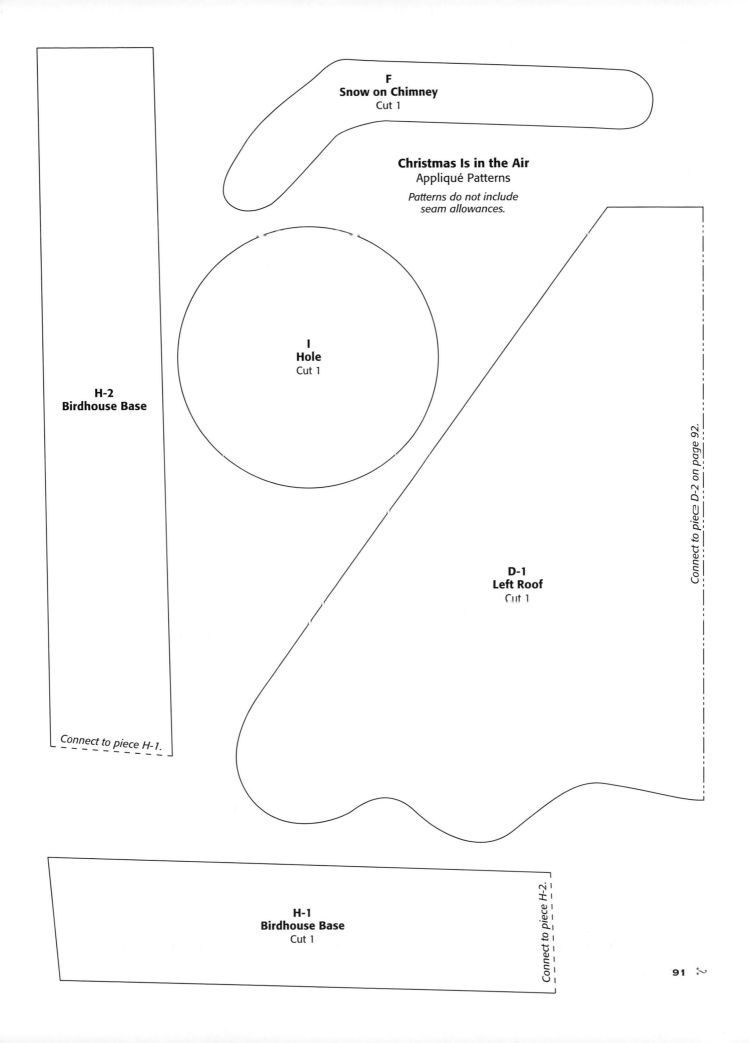

F
Snow on Chimney
Cut 1

Christmas Is in the Air
Appliqué Patterns

*Patterns do not include
seam allowances.*

I
Hole
Cut 1

H-2
Birdhouse Base

D-1
Left Roof
Cut 1

Connect to piece D-2 on page 92.

Connect to piece H-1.

H-1
Birdhouse Base
Cut 1

Connect to piece H-2.

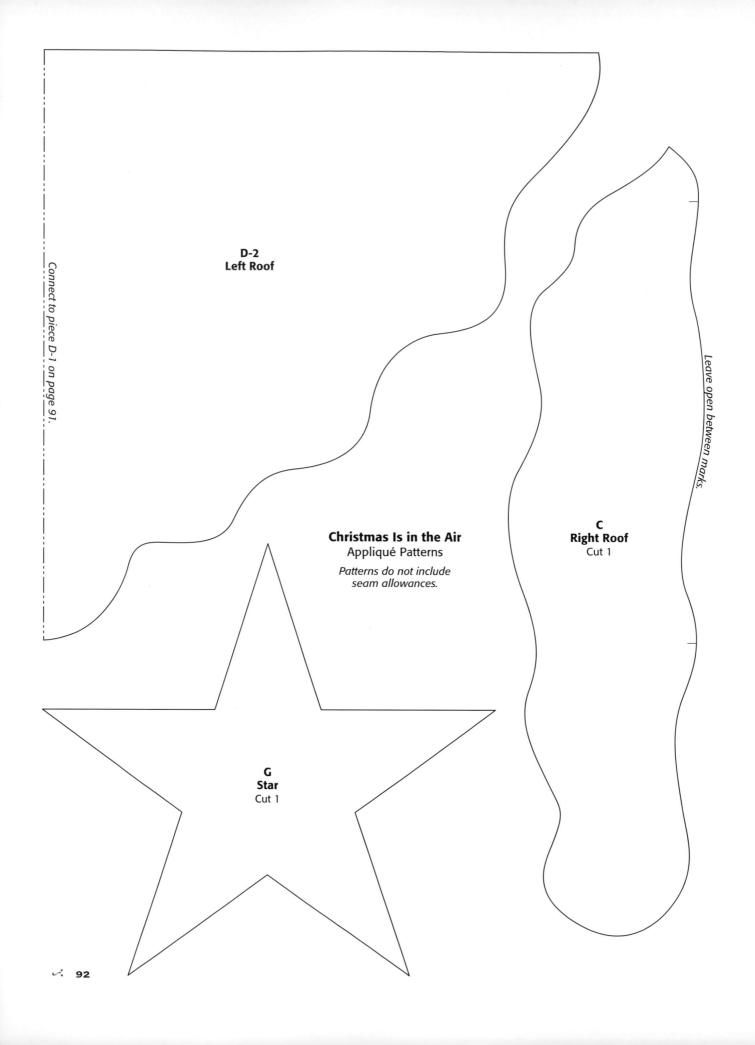

D-2
Left Roof

Connect to piece D-1 on page 91.

Christmas Is in the Air
Appliqué Patterns

*Patterns do not include
seam allowances.*

C
Right Roof
Cut 1

Leave open between marks.

G
Star
Cut 1

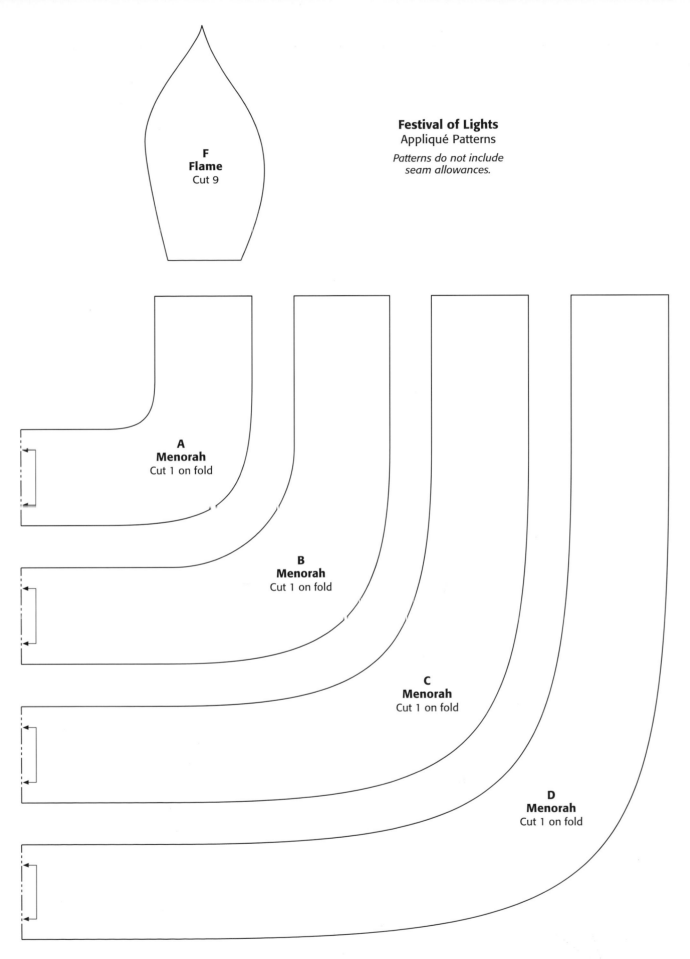

F
Flame
Cut 9

Festival of Lights
Appliqué Patterns

*Patterns do not include
seam allowances.*

A
Menorah
Cut 1 on fold

B
Menorah
Cut 1 on fold

C
Menorah
Cut 1 on fold

D
Menorah
Cut 1 on fold

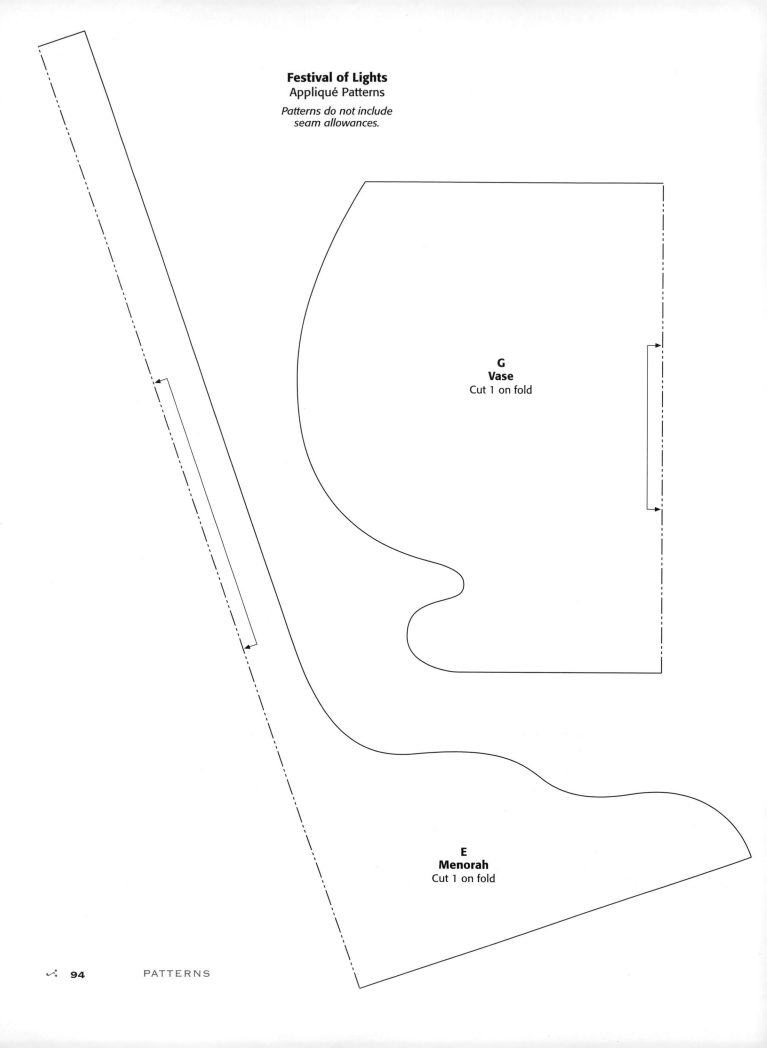

Festival of Lights
Appliqué Patterns

*Patterns do not include
seam allowances.*

G
Vase
Cut 1 on fold

E
Menorah
Cut 1 on fold

ABOUT THE AUTHOR

Photo by Steve Gold

Joanne Goldstein combines her background in art with a love for quilting. Her passion for fabric, handwork, embellishment, and design has resulted in a creative approach to contemporary quilting.

Holiday Collage Quilts is Joanne's second book that explores the possibilities of using contemporary fabrics to create dynamic fabric collages. The success of her first book, *Fabric Collage Quilts* (Martingale & Company, 1999), has given Joanne the opportunity to lecture and teach workshops across the country. She loves to show students how to create unique and impressive fabric collages by combining contemporary methods with traditional quiltmaking techniques. Her work has also been featured in *Quilter's Newsletter Magazine* and *American Quilter*.

Joanne has three grown children: Steven, Lauren, and David. She lives with her husband, Jerry, in Coral Springs, Florida.